CAREER GUIDE TO SPORTS OFFICIATING

by
R. I. ODUMS

YOU CALL THE SHOTS!

A Complete Handbook on How To Become
An Umpire, Referee, Judge or Minor Official

Library of Congress Cataloging in Publication Data

84-072743

ODUMS, R. I.
Career Guide To Sports Officiating
(You Call The Shots)

ISBN 0-936217-00-6

MANUFACTURED IN THE UNITED STATES
First Edition (Revised)

TABLE OF CONTENTS

PREFACE

Undertaking a career in officiating sports can be a very profitable and personally satisfying experience. It is also a serious decision — one that should not be taken lightly. This publication will help you make that critical decision. It will provide the reader with important insight and factual information as well as contacts for becoming a sports official in the following areas: **Baseball, softball, football, basketball, tennis, golf, ice hockey, soccer, track and field (cross country), volleyball, gymnastics, wrestling, and boxing.**

Additional information includes *Professional training schools, contact persons with telephone numbers, names and addresses of the various conferences, organizations and associations, plus a range of salaries involved for the various sports listed above.* Brief information is also provided on swimming, skiing, lacrosse, archery, cycling, canoeing, diving, fencing, figure skating, judo, roller skating, rowing, rifle shooting, speed skating, synchronized swimming, table tennis, team handball, water polo, weightlifting, yacht racing, wheelchair racing, biathlon, equestrian, pentathlon and luge.

Each major sport covered, explores the various aspects involved in becoming an official in that sport. Opportunities exist for referees, umpires, judges, chair officials, scorekeepers, timekeepers, statisticians, starter officials, goal and line judges. Because there is tremendous competition to secure these well paying positions, you must be prepared to lay the proper foundation for the occupation.

A paradox faces you when you decide to enter the sports arena. You serve in a highly visible activity; however, you are expected to maintain a low profile. You are an important element to the game, but not one of the participating players. Your ability to make fast and accurate decisions will ultimately determine whether you will succeed or fail.

This material will equip you with the crucial information needed to develop your true potential.

For years, the field of officiating sports was closed to those who lacked knowledge of the requirements and application procedures. Today, the procedures have not changed. Numerous opportunities exist in both part-time and full-time positions. You can earn up to $100,000 a year as a full-time, major league umpire or referee. Those who desire to supplement their income or work part-time, can have a weekly earning range of $150 to $300 a week.

Additional benefits can include liberal mileage and travel allowances, per diem expenses and fully paid medical insurance. To eliminate the mystery that has been kept out of the hands of sports enthusiasts such as yourself, this book takes a major step by providing you with pertinent information.

Because of new leagues being formed along with regular league expansions, more and more opportunities are being created each season, not only in the United States, but in Canada, Mexico and in many other countries.

Because the field of officiating sports is so broad and varied, most potential candidates believe the procedures and qualifications are beyond their grasp. This is not true. If you possess the ability to apply basic native talent and are willing to put forth the necessary time and effort to develop your awareness of the application procedures and qualifications, you can immediately begin pursuing a sports officiating career.

INTRODUCTION

CAREER GUIDE TO SPORTS OFFICIATING was written for the sports enthusiast who has a serious interest in beginning a career in officiating. It is designed to give basic information to the person who has no previous experience or knowledge of sports or sports officiating, as well as those who have a general knowledge of sports but not specifically in officiating. This book will assist those who have previous officiating experience and would like to advance to a higher level.

Written in simple and easy to understand language, this book provides the reader with a brief history of each sport and a general description of how the game is played, along with some facts regarding the various levels of play involved at the amateur, high school, collegiate and professional levels. Where the information is available, each chapter contains facts on economics, the number of leagues, teams and players; the number of officials utilized in games and basic facts on compensation for those who seek full- or part-time earnings.

Each chapter discusses the basic qualifications and characteristics needed to become a successful and proficient official.

The chapter entitled "Getting Started," gives step-by-step procedures for beginning a career and then advancing to different levels including the professional level.

"Golden Opportunities" illustrates the numerous opportunities available to blacks, women and other minorities once they begin to join the sports associations and federations.

The names, addresses and telephone numbers of the appropriate associations and federations are listed in various appendixes located in the back of the book.

Information on the mechanics of officiating has always been readily available through such sources as rule books, training clinics, officiating courses and associations. The information which has been previously known only to a few and which this book focuses on is the step-by-step procedure for beginning a career as an official. Therefore, mechanics are mentioned only as they relate to the overall view of the sport. Contacts for obtaining information and training on the mechanics of officiating are provided throughout the chapters and appendixes.

A great deal of time and energy has been expended gathering data and putting together a formula that will produce positive results for those serious-minded individuals. The author hopes that you are one of them.

CHAPTER I

UNDERSTANDING THE PROFESSION

A professional sports official has a multitude of responsibilities. Not only are you required to enforce the rules and control the action, you may be called upon to keep the peace. Collectively, being a highly qualified sports official is an art in itself. For those who can master this art form, the financial rewards are well worth the effort and time investment. To qualify yourself for serious consideration, you must be able to demonstrate your understanding and awareness of well-defined and basic criteria.

CHARACTERISTICS: One of the primary considerations evaluated by others is your ability to influence the appropriate field action without becoming part of it. This requires you, as the sports official, to maintain a low profile. This quality is difficult to acquire if you are prone to grandstanding or putting on a show. In fact, no matter how well you know the rules, and no matter how fast you are able to respond in a particular situation, exhibiting a character that brings too much attention to yourself as an official may be an overriding factor in having a potential official dismissed from consideration.

Another essential characteristic is self-confidence. Both players and audiences have the ability to sense when an official lacks self-confidence in the performance of his duties. This deficiency reveals itself when an official is not at the right place at the right time, or when the fairness of a decision is repeatedly brought into question. Other times, it may simply be a matter that the official does not demonstrate an understanding of the importance of a particular situation. Individually or combined, any of these characteristics may be grounds for disqualification or denial of future opportunities to participate in major events.

When a particular sporting event fails to progress in a satisfactory manner, the problem is usually the result of one or more officials failing to demonstrate knowledge of the game. Although poor sportsmanship may have been initiated by the players themselves, it is the duty of the officials to remedy the situation the moment it arises. To command respect and enforce the game rules are clearly the responsibility of the officials. When the official is plagued with lack of self-confidence, this becomes almost an insurmountable task.

PERSONAL RELATIONSHIPS: There is a professional relationship that must be maintained between players and officials. The code of conduct governing a particular sport can be interpreted within a narrow or broad band depending upon the level of the sport involved. Unfortunately, no one standard has been found to fit every situation and every sport. But the trend to achieve and maintain an air of professionalism has always been an underlying theme in officiating sports.

This, however, does not preclude proper relations when dealing with players and other sports officials. Some officials never talk to players when off the field for any reason. This eliminates the possibility of fraternizing or possible impropriety. If such behavior is carried to extremes, some players become fearful of officials, but the official earns their respect. Other officials who are more confident in their personal relationships tend to be more relaxed and open. In either case, they must have the ability to draw the line between serving in an official capacity and acting in social situations.

Each individual must follow a standard that fits his or her personality as well as the occasion. Those individuals who understand the levels of professional conduct are able to establish and maintain ideal standards in their relationships with others — no matter whom they are interacting with and no matter what the circumstances. These types of individuals are always in high demand, and their professional services command the higher rewards.

Officials who outwardly project an image of arrogance tend to arouse spectators' antagonism. At the major league level, public relations is a highly valued commodity, and poor public relations should be avoided like a social plague. Undesirable crowd activity or even poor audience attendance often affects potential earnings and advertising sponsors. Any official who contributes to poor public relations will probably have a very short career.

In general, American sports is one of the country's most important institutions attracting billions of dollars in business revenue. Thus, a positive public relations image is extremely important. Each sports official inherits this responsibility. If you think you can measure up to these standards, the rest of the qualifications will become slightly easier.

CHAPTER II

GENERAL QUALIFICATIONS FOR BECOMING AN OFFICIAL

These are general qualifications and are considered prerequisites for becoming a sports official. As you review each item, you should attempt to evaluate yourself in terms of possessing these qualities. When you have a doubt as to whether you possess the skill, knowledge and discipline required, you should seriously review your interest and ability to sufficiently reform before committing your time, effort and financial resources.

Physical Requirements:

Most sports officials are required to be physically fit to perform their obligation. In most cases, especially in professional sports, officials will be required to undergo a complete physical examination prior to the start of a season. At the professional level, simply being physically fit is not sufficient, for most of the professional leagues also require you to possess an alert and sound mind.

Active sports such as football, baseball, hockey, basketball, soccer, wrestling or boxing require the referees and umpires to be in constant motion throughout the sporting event. If one is not in top-notch physical shape, it is difficult to move quickly and be able to maintain sufficient monitoring of the players.

More than ever before, sporting events at the professional and amateur levels are being covered by national and local media. An official who is out of shape may incur the ridicule of reporters and spectators much to the detriment of the event.

Personal Qualities:

As previously stated, a sport's official must maintain a low-key profile. The audience does not come to a sporting event to watch one or more of the officials put on a show or play to the grandstand. There is a certain amount of decorum that must be maintained before, during and after the event. Any attempt not to conform within accepted standard procedures, rules or protocol is unacceptable conduct. This means that all signals, calls and procedures are to conform to a specific code of conduct, and this conduct is not subject to individual interpretation or over dramatics.

Therefore, being overly dramatic or attempting to put on a one-man show by a sports official may be sufficient grounds to have the individual removed, and in some cases, eliminated from participating in future sporting events.

Ability to Make Decisions:

Too often a novice official will make the mistake of confusing quick with hasty. True, a play call must be made quickly and positively. However, making a call when out of position usually results in a poor or questionable decision. This is another reason why it is important to be in top physical shape, as being able to move quickly is often required to be in the right position at the right time to make the right call.

Although a momentary hesitation on part of an official is not necessarily a sign of indecision, pondering too long over a decision tends to make both players and the audience question the quality of the decision. The ability to make quick and accurate decisions is a developed skill that is best acquired through practice. Developed and indeed cultivated, this ability is a valuable asset that is continuously in demand by those hiring sports officials.

Having a strong, clear voice, coupled with the ability to project it in a tone of authority, is considered by some to be just as important as knowing the rules of the game.

Knowledge of Rules:

Possessing a thorough knowledge and understanding of the rules covering a particular sporting activity improves the ability to respond quickly and accurately.

The ability to apply game rules to a particular situation must appear to be automatic. You must be able to mentally picture a play as the situation occurs so that you can recognize the correct rule to be applied. Guessing is not acceptable conduct, and the best procedure for eliminating this type of embarrassment is to know the rules thoroughly.

Learning something to a point of habit is not as easy as it may appear. Poor learning and studying habits prove most embarrassing when thousands of spectators witness your ignorance or question your competency. To avoid this situation, you should be prepared to continuously review and study the rules, including hypothetical situations covering all possible game conditions.

Mechanics:

In addition to the physical requirements, a candidate must know the mechanics and signals involved in a particular sport. Although there has been no indication that a candidate would be disqualified because of a physical handicap (such as a missing arm, leg or hand), it is reasonable to assume you would have to be able to perform the mechanics, physical handicaps notwithstanding.

Demeanor & Impartiality:

One of the most difficult tasks facing referees and umpires is ignoring remarks from spectators and fans. The larger the crowd the greater the chances that there will be those in the audience who will take every opportunity to heckle or rattle the officials. Many spectators feel it is their duty to criticize any official who steps onto the field of play. This misguided sense of false duty requires the targeted official to turn a deaf ear and ignore all spectator remarks, suggestions or comments. You must rise above any amount of name-calling, no matter how derogatory or defamatory. If you have executed the performance of your duties well, chances are the crowd will turn against the heckler(s) in your defense. On the other hand, if you have failed to execute those duties, don't expect anything other than a heightened reaction from the crowd.

An official is not only required to maintain the proper demeanor on the field but this requirement equally applies to off the field situations. You must learn to say "no comment" when asked about your views on a decision made on the field, either by yourself or a fellow sports official. Fortunately, the media is aware of this standard and usually will not approach a sports official for comments and other remarks. It should be pointed out, however, that not all reporters or commentators are knowledgeable about this code of conduct and might inadvertently approach you for your statements or remarks. This is as close to an absolute "no-no" that a sports official can commit. Any remark about another sports official — justified or not — should be strictly kept to yourself. You are not permitted the luxury of making personal comments or stating your opinions to the media.

Conduct:

Being a sports official, you will find it impossible to avoid all contact with players, and their coaches. A professional attitude, however, must prevail at all times before, during and after a sporting event. You must never argue with a player, a coach or team representative. When contact is made, any and all discussions should be kept to as few words as possible while remaining courteous and polite. Simply put, you are not afforded the luxury of arguing, and indeed are under an obligation to avoid and prevent it.

Your overall appearance must project professional qualities of excellent conduct. Proper attire must be worn, rapport with other officials must be maintained and duties must be discharged in a competent manner; these are some of the best policies a potential sports official can develop.

These qualities and abilities are not automatically acquired. They require an extensive amount of learning, and you must apply yourself to develop this overall proficiency that is best acquired through practical experience. For this reason, an extensive amount of experience must be acquired at the amateur level before applying for professional level consideration.

CHAPTER III

GETTING STARTED

This book is applicable throughout the United States. The principles and procedures contained herein are also applicable in Canada and in many other English-speaking countries as well as many non-English speaking countries. No matter what officiating career you ultimately choose, certain steps should be followed. The procedure in getting started is somewhat universal. The following steps will enhance your success and expedite your officiating career.

The **FIRST STEP,** should be to contact your local state high school athletic association. **NOTE:** Refer to **Appendix A,** which is a complete listing of all the high school athletic associations located throughout the United States.

When you have made the necessary contact with one of these athletic associations, request a) a current rule book, b) an officiating manual, c) an application and the application procedure governing the specific sport, and d) request a list of recommended officiating schools or approved training agencies in your region. **NOTE:** You may also refer to **Appendix E,** which is a list of private officiating schools and accredited collegiate-level officiating courses.

The **SECOND STEP** is to contact area recreational directors or the physical education instructors with the local facilities. This should be done so that you may observe and volunteer to officiate with community programs, at the intramural program at a local junior high or high school, or with a local church or synagogue league. Your involvement will provide an invaluable opportunity to acquire practical experience. Even at this level, some of the organizations will provide fees or salaries. Experience, however, will be the most important factor!

After you have acquired some practical experience (one to three seasons), you are ready for the **THIRD STEP.** Now you are in the position to command more compensation from the various local recreational organizations, intramural programs, youth leagues, religious organizations, and most importantly interscholastic competition at the junior and high school levels. You should be mentally and physically prepared to perform at this level of competition for at least five seasons of major high school sports and five seasons at a small college. It is at this level where your performance evaluations will determine whether or not there will be advancement in your officiating career.

The **FOURTH STEP** is to seek acceptance on the collegiate and/or semi-professional level. It will be necessary for you to secure letters of recommendation from local recreational directors, other officials, intramural directors, league officials and area junior high/high school athletic directors. Thus, your earlier contact with these individuals becomes important in determining whether you will advance in your career. Letters of recommendation should refer to your character, ability, past work experiences relating to officiating and interests in being an official. Letters of recommendation are absolutely required to work at the collegiate level and most of the semi-pro levels.

After you have secured a reasonable number of letters of recommendation, you can approach the National Collegiate Athletic Association for membership and additional ratings. You will be tested as to the level of your proficiency. When you have made the necessary contact with the NCAA, NAIA or the CFA, request a) a current rule book, b) an officiating manual, c) the application procedure governing the specific sport, and d) a list of recommended officiating schools or approved training agencies or clinics in your region. **NOTE:** Refer to **Appendix B,** which is a list of college conferences and associations. Refer to **Appendix E,** which is a list of private officiating schools and accredited collegiate-level officiating courses.

Semi-pro leagues and their officials are sometimes difficult to locate. However, your local sports reporter can easily provide you with a sufficient number of leads pertaining to semi-pro organizations because such reporters are constantly required to cover their events.

STEP FIVE: Professional officiating at the major league level is the most difficult to achieve, because you have to be selected and invited to participate. As a general rule, you need at least ten years of practical experience, five of which are usually acquired at the collegiate and/or semi-pro level. Although this time frame may appear lengthy, the time and effort is well worth the eventual financial reward. Also, your memberships in officiating organizations are given serious consideration. Therefore, it is important for you to have gained enrollment with one or more accredited officials' associations as soon as possible. **NOTE:** A cross-section of these professional organizations found in Appendix C. **HINT: Enroll in one or more of the sport's officiating camps** (training schools). Evaluations are regularly conducted, and these camps are regularly visited by scouts or recruiters who are seeking top-level officiating talent. In most cases, the camp's director or coordinator will select and recommend potential candidates for professional openings. **Note: Appendix E** is a list of private officiating schools.

An exception to the above guidelines, is that a former professional player of major league sports or a collegiate coach may not need the full ten years of experience.

As a general policy with professional major league officiating, you will be requested to forward at least three letters of recommendation from recognized authorities. These include coaches, managers, collegiate athletic directors, sports commissioners, referee supervisors and umpires. The letters will allow them to conduct a preliminary investigation to determine your officiating potential. Then, an application is forwarded to you for completion. In addition, a copy of your application is provided to one of the area observers or scouts for a follow-up visual evaluation and report. The results of this report-evaluation will ultimately determine your final career destiny.

With both professional and amateur sports, specific guidelines and standards have been established to ensure uniform proficiency, fairness and effectiveness. You must be willing to acquire the necessary knowledge, experience and technique to demonstrate your ability to meet this basic criteria.

Successful gamesmanship often depends upon the quality of the officials participating in the event. Their overall knowledge of the rules, command of the mechanical requirements and ability to interpret field of play situations (good judgment), are the necessary qualities each official must possess. Anything less would be a disservice to the profession and individual sport involved.

This material does not cover every possible sports situation, but it will provide the interested reader with a thorough understanding of the minimum requirements and what it takes to become a successful sports official.

If you are interested in becoming a sports official such as an umpire, referee, judge, starter, field official, linesman, chair official, meet coordinator, clerk of courts, games committee person, time keeper or score keeper, this material will prove a valuable asset in obtaining your occupational goal. As in most careers in professional sports, gaining entrance into the field requires perseverance, study and work. For those who are willing to put forth the necessary time and energy, the rewards are worth the efforts.

Near the end of this material, you will also find additional appendixes that will enhance your knowledge. **Appendix D** will provide you with a list of sports publications and periodicals, and **Appendix F** deals with the major sports equipment manufacturers and suppliers that can provide you with the professional image.

Application Procedures:

As stated, to apply for an application for becoming a licensed sports official, you must write to your local state high school athletic association. If you are not in possession of a current official's handbook, rule book and case book pertaining to your specific sport, request that material from the association. Usually there will be a nominal fee.

Each sport has an official high school rule book, case book or official's manual. You must acquire a current edition for study purposes. Should your state's association be unable to provide you with current manuals to study, you can easily obtain up-to-date information by writing to this address:

The National Federation
Of State High School Associations
11724 Plaza Circle
P. O. Box 20626
Kansas City, MO 64195

Individual state applications, however, are provided by the individual states. Therefore, to request a specific application, you would address your request to the state's high school athletic association. (See Appendix A at the back of the book for the location nearest you.)

You will be forwarded an instruction sheet which should be reviewed carefully. In addition, another sheet will be included indicating when and where the official examinations covering specific sports will be held. The third sheet will be the application itself.

The application is easy to complete, but do not underestimate its importance just because it is not difficult. The application applies to several categories and levels of officiating sports. As long as you adhere to the instructions outlined, there will be little or no difficulty in completing the application correctly.

Even a minor error can delay your successful application processing for an entire year, because many of the tests are only administered annually.

Make sure you have included the application fee with the application. This usually is a minimal amount, but again, an application can be rejected or delayed if a fee was requested and not enclosed.

CHAPTER IV

REGULATIONS FOR BEING AN OFFICIAL

Virtually all sports officials are required to be licensed. It would be impossible to cover all of the regulation procedures that exist on all the various levels of play. We have therefore elected to focus on the regulation procedures on the high school level. For information on the regulation procedures of the various collegiate and professional levels, write directly to the appropriate association listed in Appendixes B and C.

The licensing of high school officials is primarily controlled by the state's High School Athletic Association. The association is governed by a board of directors who determine the licensing, training and testing procedures.

In making their determinations, these directors place heavy emphasis upon an individual's moral character, integrity and lack of prejudices. Should an error be made in determining these qualities, the state's Athletic Association has the authority to suspend any official based upon poor conduct (on or off the field), demonstrated biases (as to race, religion) or deterioration in physical or mental fitness. In addition, individual State Charters usually have the authority to suspend an official for non-payment of licensing fees, not attending scheduled meetings or wearing attire other than that which has been specifically prescribed by the state's High School Athletic Association.

Each state will have a prescribed procedure for meeting and maintaining its requirements. The individual bears complete responsibility for complying with these procedures at all times.

For example, moving from one district to another within a state will require you to notify the District Secretary of the Association and register your new address to receive announcements of meetings. Failure or delay in performing this otherwise simple task may eventually lead to suspension.

Examination:

If you are a candidate (or applicant) for a particular sport and have no previous experience as a licensed official, you will be required to take a written examination.

Although many of the examinations are "open book" tests, an hour in duration, do not rely upon this. Open book examinations tend to be more difficult than closed book examinations because of problems in locating the exact answer. Therefore, it is strongly recommended you know the material thoroughly before you attempt to take the examination.

In addition to completing the examination successfully, you must fill out an application form correctly and completely. Be sure to inspect the reverse side of the application form, where a witnessed signature is required.

In most situations, the application must be completed prior to taking the examination and will require you to specify where the examination is being taken and exactly which sport examination is being requested. Different examinations are given for baseball and softball for example.

An application fee is usually required, and if so, be prepared to have it enclosed with the application. Usually this fee is nonrefundable.

The examination for a particular sport is usually administered once each year. The exact time and location for these examinations can be obtained by writing to the state's High School Athletic Association for their exam schedule. Arranging to take the test on an earlier date and time is difficult. Unless you have an *excellent* reason, the chances are very unlikely that an exception will be made.

Basic eligibility will require you to be at least 18 years of age (or older) and not enrolled in a high school curriculum.

After you have successfully completed the examination, including application and fee requirements, you will be given "temporary" or "registered" rating status in a particular sport such as volleyball, football, soccer, field hockey, baseball, softball, basketball, ice hockey, gymnastics, wrestling, track and field, or swimming and diving.

Transferring your license from one state to another in the event of relocation, will require you to notify the state's High School Athletic Association within a 90-day period. Then, if there exists a reciprocity agreement between the two states, and you are able to present documented evidence that you hold a valid license as a sport's official in the previous state, merely filing the new state's application accompanied with the appropriate application fee will usually suffice. In the event no reciprocity agreement exists between the new and previous state, you will have to repeat the entire licensing process again.

Each state's Athletic Association will require you to attend a minimum number of meetings at the local and regional levels. This number will vary depending upon the sport involved, but usually the minimum requirement is four meetings a year for each sport in which you desire to maintain a license. Failure to register your attendance can result in either a suspension of your license, a fine or both.

Special Training:

Adult education classes for becoming a licensed sports official when properly sponsored by area colleges, high schools or officials representing the state's Athletic Association are recommended, though not technically required.

Do not confuse optional training with required associational meetings conducted at the regional or state levels. Attendance at these meetings is required in order to maintain knowledge and proficiency.

Official Ratings:

State licensing ratings are issued in one of two categories -as either Temporary or Registered status. Either rating allows the holder to officiate junior high school or high school athletic events.

The Temporary Rating allows the official to apply for and acquire advancement to a Registered Rating after acquiring two years practical experience (or in the case of an official transferring from out of state, one year additional experience providing there has been one year's experience already acquired).

Registered Rating status is usually not automatic. Registered status requires two years (or sport seasons) experience gained in each sport in which one holds a Temporary status.

In addition, the candidate will be required to pass a closed book examination covering the rules and regulations of the sport. Generally, a higher passing score is required than for a Temporary Rating.

In the event the particular sport requires a mechanics examination (such as in football, basketball and baseball), this additional examination will immediately follow the written examination. Again, a higher passing score is usually required than for a Temporary Rating.

Each candidate must receive at least two favorable reports from other Registered Rated or qualified retired officials. These qualified officials must physically observe your performance during a scheduled event. Furthermore, these otherwise qualified officials must not be participating in the event other than serving in an observer capacity. In other words, observations and reports made by officials who were also officiating the event would not be acceptable.

Special Exception:

Officiating girls gymnastics is governed under a different set of rules and procedures. Prior to being eligible for a High School Athletic Association's license, the candidate must first apply for a rating through the United States Gymnastics Federation Judging Program. This application procedure is a prerequisite, and is not handled by the individual state's High School Athletic Association's board or secretary.

Restrictions Involving Varsity Football and Basketball:

Temporary Rated officials are not generally permitted to officiate varsity football and varsity basketball. Only in the event of an emergency which would prevent a Registered Rated official from participating would a Temporary Rated official be utilized. In such an event, joint prior approval from the high schools involved and the state's High School Athletic Association must be granted.

Penalties:

Violations of rules and procedures are both costly and time consuming ordeals. Any official who is not qualified by license (or rating status) can be heavily fined and placed on a one year's probation. Furthermore, all future officiating can be halted until the fine is paid in full, and any contracts entered into or held can be declared void.

Sufficient penalties have been implemented to discourage even small infractions of the rules and regulations. These regularly include probation, suspension, written or verbal reprimand and even censure if the violation is serious.

When a suspension penalty is imposed, generally it will be initiated by the District Officials Committee and is subject to an appeals process. This procedure is best avoided, and proper conduct is one of the best policies an official possesses.

Official Uniforms:

No matter how just your cause, strong your beliefs or morally founded your feelings, a strict dress code is always required. This means that no emblems, signs, insignia or patches of any kind, form or shape can be displayed on your official's uniform other than those specifically authorized by the state's High School Athletic Association. Do not waste your time or energy seeking an exception or special approval — it will not be considered. The Code of Regulations and individual By Laws issued to the licensing associations make no provisions to allow anyone the authority to grant you permission.

All dress and color codes are to be strictly observed. This usually includes everything that is visible. Each sport has an official uniform code. There is little, and in some cases, no leeway allowed in conforming to these requirements.

CHAPTER V

GOLDEN OPPORTUNITIES
(for Blacks, Women and Other Minorities)

Until recently, the "ranks" of sports officials did not include blacks, women or other minorities. Minorities are now starting to realize the GOLDEN OPPORTUNITIES that exist for them in officiating.

Blacks, Hispanics and women are now being called upon to officiate from the high school level to the major leagues. Nevertheless there is still a disproportionately low number of minorities officiating. For example, as of 1982, the National Basketball Association (NBA) had a total of five black officials and no women, although women referees are officiating women's basketball on the collegiate level. The North American Soccer League (NASL) had only one woman official and no blacks; the National Football League (NFL) had 11 blacks and one woman, while both the United States Football League (USFL) and the Canadian Football League (CFL) had no women or blacks.

In the past, minorities were eliminated from consideration partly because of some form of discrimination (race or sex). The organizations are now making an affirmative effort to correct the disparity in the number of minority officials.

Golden Opportunities exist from the moment minorities elect to join the "ranks" of the various sports associations. Minorities can no longer stay on the outside if they expect to advance. The moment they elect to become an active participant in sports federations and associations is the moment they realize the golden opportunities. This is the KEY to opening up the locked doors to these employment opportunities.

As repeatedly indicated, each state has its own high school athletic association. Many of these associations are affiliated with interlocking local, regional, national and international sports associations. These federations and associations are the controlling factor in determining selection and ultimate career path. Without membership, you will go nowhere!

Each association has its own qualifications and time restrictions. As soon as possible, you must join as many federations and sports associations as are relevant to your officiating interest. The majority of these organizations are understaffed with respect to qualified minorities, and the organizers regularly seek out their applications. For example, as of 1984, the Amateur Hockey Association of the United States (AHAUS) had 9,500 registered officials with 27 affiliated associations throughout the United States, but only 8% of the officials are women and even fewer Blacks. As of 1982, professional major league baseball had only two women umpires both in the minor league, and only one active black umpire (two are retired), in the major league's 107-year history.

Walking up the employment ladder from amateur competition to collegiate play to international sports and finally to the professional major-league level will require membership in the appropriate federations, organizations and associations.

A cross-section of these professional and semi-professional associations should provide you with the depth and magnitude of the opportunities available. Randomly listed below are some of the associations with golden opportunities available for minorities in sports officiating.

- **Amateur Softball Association of America (ASA)** has 65,000 registered umpires that govern 150,000 teams. It should be realized that more than 31 million people play softball throughout the United States as of 1984. This is an excellent starting point for anyone interested in softball or baseball. (See chapter on baseball/softball).

- **The International Association of Approved Basketball Officials (IAABO)** has more than 13,000 registered officials with 200 area boards governing high school and college basketball throughout the United States as of 1984. NOTE: 5% are females. Opportunities are numerous for IAABO members. (See chapter on basketball).

- **The Amateur Hockey Association of the United States (AHAUS)** has more than 9,500 registered officials and are affiliated with 27 associations throughout the United States. NOTE: 8% are women as of 1984. There are tremendous opportunities for both women and other minorities. (See chapter on ice hockey.)

- **United States Soccer Federation (USSF), North American Soccer League (NASL)** and the **Canadian Soccer Association**

(CSA) have more than 100 registered officials. NOTE: 2% are females, and few Blacks and Latins. (See chapter on soccer).

- **The National Federation of State High School Associations (NFIOA)** has multiple membership organizations and covers nine states: Indiana (8,000 officials), South Carolina (1,550 officials), Louisiana (3,000 officials), Arkansas (1,900 officials), Colorado (2,000 officials), Utah (1,100 officials), Arizona (2,000 officials), Idaho (1,200 officials) and Alaska (500 officials). This federation covers all high school sports, and is well known in these states as the "Manditory Nine." Each of these states has its own high school athletic association, but in order to officiate within these states at the high school and college levels, you must be a member of both. When you join the high school athletic association, part of the membership fee will be applied to your membership in NFIOA.

- **The National Association for Girls and Women in Sports/ Affiliated Board of Officials (NAGWS/ABO)** has 5,000 rated basketball officials, and 1,700 women's basketball teams in the United States abide by the organization's rules and utilize NAGWS officials. (See chapter on basketball).

- **The United States Tennis Association (USTA)** has more than 18,000 certified officials throughout the country. NOTE: 40% are females. (See chapter on tennis)

- **Western College Official Bureau and Fermar Corporation of North California Association of College Officials** independently contract their members to high schools and colleges in California. The organization supplies officials for: basketball, football, water polo, girls' field hockey, soccer, softball, baseball and volleyball.

- **The Ohio High School Athletic Association** is divided into districts, but maintains more than 10,800 registered officials that cover the full range of sporting events at the high school level. NOTE: Each state is listed in Appendix A.

The above organizations are only a few of the more than 100 associations that have open membership. Every state has at least one such organization, and most states have several. Reminder: For telephone numbers, addresses and specific contacts, see Appendix C, Professional Associations and Organizations.

The opportunities will continue to expand for qualified officials at all levels because the world has gone sPoRtS cRaZy! New leagues and associations are being formed regularly throughout the United States,

Canada, Europe and Japan. The staggering list of participants at the present time will increase and perhaps double in the next 10 to 15 years based upon the present rate of growth. The listings that follow on the number of participants should provide you with some idea of the need and opportunities.

Total player participation in the six major professional sports is approximately 276 (NBA), 480 (NLB), 560 (ALB), 171 (NASL), 1,372 (NFL), 1,500 (USTA) and 630 (NHL) for a combined total of 4,989, according to the public relation departments from each sport.

At the collegiate level, the total number of varsity player participants in the NCAA, CFA and NAIA is 375,349.

The total number of amateurs participating in major and minor sports is in excess of 125 million.

According to the National Federation of State High School Athletic Associations sports participation survey for 1983, more than 6 million boys and girls compete in various sports on the high school level. The following charts are a state-by-state breakdown on the number of participants per sport. The indications from these charts are clear, there exist a magnitude of opportunities available on the high school level alone.

These statistics merely reflect high school participation, and do not include the myriad participants that are competing at the junior high, recreational centers, YM-YWCAs and private club facilities. As you can see, the golden opportunities for qualified officials are too numerous to cover.

Now, add to this participation the games played by professionals, semi-professionals, collegiate, amateur, industrial and church leagues, and you begin to grasp the magnitude and potential that can be realized and achieved. The trend that has developed over the last two years alone, strongly indicates an expanding and financially rewarding future.

TEN MOST POPULAR BOYS SPORTS

SCHOOLS			PARTICIPANTS		
1.	Basketball	16,930	1.	Football	923,780
2.	Track	14,414	2.	Basketball	514,791
3.	Football	14,086	3.	Track	475,229
4.	Baseball	13,380	4.	Baseball	409,970
5.	Cross Country	9,581	5.	Wrestling	254,581
6.	Golf	9,062	6.	Cross Country	165,114
7.	Tennis	8,691	7.	Soccer	162,504
8.	Wrestling	8,272	8.	Tennis	126,458
9.	Soccer	4,454	9.	Golf	115,187
10.	Aquatics	3,650	10.	Aquatics	76,657

TEN MOST POPULAR GIRLS SPORTS

SCHOOLS			PARTICIPANTS		
1.	Basketball	16,417	1.	Basketball	401,511
2.	Track	13,957	2.	Track	355,652
3.	Volleyball	11,479	3.	Volleyball	269,049
4.	Tennis	8,271	4.	Softball	188,801
5.	Cross Country	7,722	5.	Tennis	120,869
6.	Softball	7,528	6.	Cross Country	93,788
7.	Aquatics	3,497	7.	Aquatics	76,261
8.	Golf	3,250	8.	Soccer	57,921
9.	Gymnastics	2,497	9.	FHockey	51,076
10.	Soccer	2,030	10.	Gymnastics	45,736

BOYS PARTICIPATION

STATE	Baseball Schools	Baseball Partic	Basketball Schools	Basketball Partic	Football Schools	Football Partic
Alabama	340	6,406	389	8,456	361	16,225
Alaska			89	1,786	15	1,052
Arizona	133	5,434	146	5,027	125	11,297
Arkansas	189	3,686	399	8,690	210	9,601
California	1,003	34,528	1,027	36,490	843	80,060
Colorado	192	5,952	260	10,400	193	11,580
Connecticut	180	5,958	180	4,752	127	7,656
Delaware	39	1,292	40	1,267	37	2,485
D.C.	13	350	15	480	14	725
Florida	398	10,622	432	12,215	356	31,918
Georgia	315	8,614	338	11,164	308	26,765
Hawaii	51	1,474	53	1,521	45	3,378
Idaho	47	1,305	125	3,641	108	6,005
Illinois	614	21,050	731	26,661	535	45,834
Indiana	391	12,450	396	13,855	318	23,000
Iowa	486	12,546	492	15,238	432	24,516
Kansas	64	2,113	370	1,067	286	14,148
Kentucky	272	5,440	284	5,680	201	7,005
Louisiana	284	7,100	412	11,516	278	12,510
Maine	132	2,508	136	4,760	61	2,440
Maryland	153	4,605	153	4,599	144	11,170
Mass	319	11,135	328	11,254	260	18,099
Michigan	638	22,357	706	25,442	635	48,191
Minnesota	375	9,953	496	12,855	364	20,660
Mississippi	219	4,645	272	5,191	245	10,940
Missouri	369	9,742	556	17,767	327	22,909
Montana			182	4,685	76	4,557
Nebraska	30	1,081	367	9,376	201	8,663
Nevada	43	1,194	61	1,840	49	3,700
N. Hamp.	83	2,500	83	2,600	33	1,800
N. Jersey	383	16,237	388	13,139	349	27,044
N. Mexico	75	2,043	126	3,602	88	4,967
New York	740	25,203	754	23,619	571	41,523
N. Carolina	329	9,182	336	9,764	320	22,508
N. Dakota	40	636	237	4,986	58	2,863
Ohio	756	21,145	804	18,829	727	38,418
Oklahoma	399	8,398	489	10,269	278	14,089
Oregon	205	9,225	251	9,036	194	12,610
Penn	572	17,900	644	19,150	560	41,020
Rhode Is.	44	1,298	44	1,132	40	1,890
S. Carolina	195	4,615	209	6,316	204	16,957

BOYS PARTICIPATION (con't)

STATE	Baseball		Basketball		Football	
	Schools	Partic	Schools	Partic	Schools	Partic
S. Dakota			204	5,284	71	3,814
Tennessee	307	7,368	350	9,800	303	19,848
Texas	747	38,385	1,140	55,350	959	77,505
Utah	86	2,191	99	3,049	82	6,394
Vermont	44	1,313	48	1,378	18	1,306
Virginia	276	8,280	286	8,550	271	21,680
Washington	281	8,078	341	10,779	281	19,008
W. Virginia	149	3,140	167	4,919	149	8,577
Wisconsin	380	9,293	422	13,715	402	28,140
Wyoming			73	1,850	62	2,100

STATE	Cross Country		Gymnastics		Ice Hockey	
	Schools	Partic	Schools	Partic	Schools	Partic
Alabama	74	649				
Alaska	72	772	1	5	15	447
Arizona	99	1,562	11	90		
Arkansas	62	310	5	20		
California	850	17,170	43	1,054		
Colorado	128	2,560	36	900	14	196
Connecticut	164	2,713			47	1,120
Delaware	30	493	1	10	1	20
D.C.	9	225				
Florida	282	3,404				
Georgia	173	2,378	11	156		
Hawaii	48	732	2	9		
Idaho	51	687				
Illinois	401	8,266	57	1,707	4	200
Indiana	384	5,940	15	245		
Iowa	243	2,900				
Kansas	194	2,361	11	146		
Kentucky	158	2,290	10	200		
Louisiana	127	1,440	19	228		
Maine	125	1,125			17	340
Maryland	124	2,062	24	282		
Mass	270	4,785	31	491	208	7,325
Michigan	488	7,828	5	79	94	2,027
Minnesota	228	3,645	20	638	148	4,898
Mississippi	39	396				
Missouri	221	4,307	8	130		
Montana	72	926	16	181		
Nebraska	139	1,495	21	181		

BOYS PARTICIPATION (con't)

STATE	Cross Country Schools	Cross Country Partic	Gymnastics Schools	Gymnastics Partic	Ice Hockey Schools	Ice Hockey Partic
Nevada	31	600				
N. Hamp.	50	1,200	5	50	22	660
N. Jersey	321	6,346	12	90		
N. Mexico	60	1,055	12	90		
New York	543	10,368	48	790	80	2,055
N. Carolina	162	2,640				
N. Dakota	41	406			13	340
Ohio	624	8,853	32	161	39	830
Oklahoma	95	1,116				
Oregon	185	2,775				
Penn	427	7,695	26	408	14	405
Rhode Is.	36	754			27	788
S. Carolina	58	832				
S. Dakota	103	1,045				
Tennessee	133	931				
Texas	571	19,550				
Utah	69	1,153				
Vermont	31	427			15	326
Virginia	193	2,895	21	210		
Washington	225	4,915	12	222		
W. Virginia	58	864				
Wisconsin	287	5,023	14	210	35	1,050
Wyoming	23	250	4	30		

STATE	Golf Schools	Golf Partic	Soccer Schools	Soccer Partic	Tennis Schools	Tennis Partic
Alabama	101	756	30	917	116	1,014
Alaska			5	246	6	122
Arizona	76	957	28	940	88	1,482
Arkansas	94	565	7	165	118	945
California	485	5,993	633	22,766	735	14,488
Colorado	96	1,152	66	1,650	93	1,674
Connecticut	170	2,045	161	5,924	137	1,650
Delaware	23	255	30	1,273	26	355
D.C.			5	125	11	165
Florida	264	2,169	262	7,563	287	2,568
Georgia	123	1,890	112	4,222	297	3,027
Hawaii	41	280	35	789	46	511

BOYS PARTICIPATION (con't)

STATE	Golf Schools	Golf Partic	Soccer Schools	Soccer Partic	Tennis Schools	Tennis Partic
Idaho	45	662			39	569
Illinois	356	6,166	166	9,245	279	5,614
Indiana	352	4,300			277	4,600
Iowa	356	5,042			110	1,596
Kansas	182	2,730	13	472	125	1,669
Kentucky	180	1,635	53	1,305	173	1,720
Louisiana	207	1,449	12	134	138	828
Maine	70	450	101	3,030	61	671
Maryland	105	918	145	5,477	138	1,774
Mass	208	2,697	256	10,373	215	2,850
Michigan	444	5,787	114	3,525	342	6,192
Minnesota	274	3,922	66	3,712	155	3,049
Mississippi	58	408	25	578	104	800
Missouri	185	2,488	81	3,240	154	2,658
Montana	46	511			41	453
Nebraska	152	1,997			43	532
Nevada	29	305	20	650	22	200
N. Hamp.	30	350	62	2,000	35	350
N. Jersey	242	3,080	340	15,167	301	4,381
N. Mexico	45	464	25	664	45	492
New York	455	5,502	558	24,080	518	8,170
N. Carolina	226	2,566	84	2,392	242	3,190
N. Dakota	69	843			22	281
Ohio	597	7,009	213	6,754	441	6,527
Oklahoma	136	1,224			108	1,104
Oregon	112	896	70	2,100	115	920
Penn	384	4,230	238	7,955	338	5,000
Rhode Is.	33	372	41	1,389	33	503
S. Carolina	118	1,183	58	1,978	116	1,349
S. Dakota	46	529			19	298
Tennessee	200	2,220			199	3,582
Texas	870	17,395			1,042	16,014
Utah	59	793	40	1,136	72	927
Vermont	20	206	42	1,338	13	151
Virginia	193	1,930	134	3,350	222	2,220
Washington	150	1,786	115	3,699	201	3,147
W. Virginia	90	925	8	181	71	741
Wisconsin	265	3,975			161	3,220
Wyoming	20	200			11	110

BOYS PARTICIPATION (con't)

STATE	Swimming/ Diving		Track/Field (indoor)		Track/Field (outdoor)	
	Schools	Partic	Schools	Partic	Schools	Partic
Alabama	19	165	72	881	208	3,598
Alaska	21	309			38	698
Arizona	38	919	137	5,802		
Arkansas	17	255	30	210	276	5,522
California	509	11,882			965	41,401
Colorado	84	2,510			250	10,000
Connecticut	81	1,860	54	2,036	167	6,391
Delaware	16	303	6	167	31	1,202
D.C.	7	250	12	501	12	682
Florida	204	2,970			347	9,785
Georgia	52	595			312	9,414
Hawaii	30	364			51	1,867
Idaho					123	3,237
Illinois	149	4,421	1	41	598	22,579
Indiana	169	4,100			386	13,000
Iowa	55	1,242			477	13,805
Kansas	28	240			375	9,679
Kentucky	25	305			213	3,723
Louisiana	33	335			352	7,040
Maine	30	450	35	630	111	3,441
Maryland	31	724	95	2,270	137	4,819
Mass	86	1,600	135	4,465	248	10,430
Michigan	230	5,489			653	24,813
Minnesota	110	2,355			419	11,467
Mississippi					206	3,825
Missouri	52	1,361			419	14,792
Montana	15	188			182	3,335
Nebraska	32	600			364	8,322
Nevada	20	150			58	1,500
N. Hamp.			20	400	45	2,000
N. Jersey	118	2,129	163	5,476	343	13,820
N. Mexico	23	333			123	3,214
New York	264	6,338	230	6,915	589	22,882
N. Carolina	38	585	41	553	284	11,002
N. Dakota	9	183			201	3,071
Ohio	192	2,978			751	25,635
Oklahoma	45	576			328	5,078
Oregon	68	1,020			240	12,000
Penn	201	4,560			503	20,000
Rhode Is.	15	373	18	771	39	1,830

BOYS PARTICIPATION (con't)

STATE	Swimming/ Diving		Track/Field (indoor)		Track/Field (outdoor)	
	Schools	Partic	Schools	Partic	Schools	Partic
S. Carolina			2	9	181	6,335
S. Dakota					204	4,926
Tennessee					198	6,138
Texas	237	4,451			1,124	45,456
Utah	38	875			97	3,047
Vermont			3	47	26	897
Virginia	41	820	102	2,550	270	9,450
Washington	94	2,251			315	9,988
W. Virginia	2	23			114	3,198
Wisconsin	97	2,910			388	13,580
Wyoming	25	300	73	1,315		

STATE	Wrestling		Skiing (downhill)		Volleyball	
	Schools	Partic	Schools	Partic	Schools	Partic
Alabama	48	1,014			11	135
Alaska	58	837			18	142
Arizona	122	4,564				
California	650	20,777	21	582	113	3,725
Colorado	202	7,676	8	96		
Connecticut	84	2,466				
Delaware	34	961			1	25
D.C.	5	125				
Florida	206	5,791				
Georgia	172	4,646				
Hawaii	39	1,095			36	520
Idaho	81	2,303				
Illinois	378	15,904				
Indiana	312	10,100				
Iowa	319	9,297				
Kansas	164	4,691				
Kentucky	58	1,102				
Louisiana	42	560				
Maine	44	792	35	420		
Maryland	133	3,928				
Mass	114	3,160	39	791		
Michigan	424	12,743	76	1,107		
Minnesota	329	8,129	42	843		
Mississippi	1	11			2	35
Missouri	164	6,376			6	92

BOYS PARTICIPATION (con't)

STATE	Wrestling Schools	Wrestling Partic	Skiing (downhill) Schools	Skiing (downhill) Partic	Volleyball Schools	Volleyball Partic
Nebraska	196	4,242				
Nevada	37	1,040	12	200		
N. Hamp.	15	450	32	550		
N. Jersey	322	11,452	15	197		
N. Mexico	44	1,416				
New York	516	17,561	74	1,521	81	1,599
N. Carolina	207	6,045				
N. Dakota	64	1,406				
Ohio	567	18,954				
Oklahoma	138	2,836			56	504
Oregon	170	4,250				
Penn	491	15,980			90	1,534
Rhode Is.	30	1,000				
S. Carolina	77	2,363				
S. Dakota	97	2,326				
Tennessee	92	2,583				
Utah	88	3,054				
Vermont	11	238	17	249		
Virginia	188	4,700				
Washington	233	7,409				
W. Virginia	86	2,068				
Wisconsin	366	12,810			34	680
Wyoming	54	1,350	7	150		

MISC. SPORTS

SPORT	STATE	SCHOOLS	PARTIC
Archery	Alaska	1	7
	New York	11	124
Badminton	California	137	2,721
	New York	14	99
Bowling	Alabama	1	15
	Georgia	1	10
	Hawaii	31	329
	Illinois	1	10
	Iowa	45	692
	Michigan	4	62
	Nevada	12	250
	New Jersey	152	2,002

BOYS PARTICIPATION (con't)
MISC. SPORTS

SPORT	STATE	SCHOOLS	PARTIC
	New York	291	3,540
	Pennsylvania	56	590
	South Carolina	9	82
	Vermont	1	20
Canoeing (crew)	Hawaii	14	179
	Delaware	1	60
	Michigan	3	119
	West Virginia	1	25
Curling	Alabama	16	58
(decathlon)	Arkansas	25	47
	Florida	34	129
	Tennessee	22	26
Fencing	Illinois	2	24
	Kentucky	5	40
	New Jersey	17	370
	New York	14	266
Field Hockey	Minnesota	113	2,740
	North Dakota	92	2,171
	South Dakota	112	2,835
	Montana	5	75
	Nebraska	6	90
	Texas	65	1,251
Judo	Hawaii	17	234
Lacrosse	Delaware	2	40
	Maryland	57	2,733
	Massachusetts	25	1,559
	New Hampshire	1	25
	New Jersey	23	1,493
	New York	161	9,852
	Virginia	3	75
Riflery	Alaska	13	195
	Georgia	39	520
	Hawaii	8	122
	Illinois	1	28
	Kentucky	17	104
	Massachusetts	6	85
	Michigan	1	4
	New York	67	954
	Pennsylvania	53	728
Skiing	Alaska	35	402
(cross-country)	Maine	42	252

BOYS PARTICIPATION
MISC. SPORTS (con't)

	Minnesota	61	920
	New Hampshire	32	550
	Vermont	19	194
	Wyoming	7	150
Softball Fast	Missouri	25	400
Softball Slow	Alabama	4	73
	Georgia	8	123
	Mississippi	6	99
Squash and	California	311	7,546
Water Polo	Florida	18	254
	Hawaii	5	84
	Illinois	6	149
	Michigan	6	121
	Missouri	14	378
	Nevada	1	12
	Utah	7	131
Weightlifting	Florida	95	2,189
	Georgia	30	1,899
	North Carolina	12	286
	South Carolina	8	137
	Utah	9	257

GIRLS PARTICIPATION

STATE	Basketball Schools	Basketball Partic	Cross Country Schools	Cross Country Partic	Field Hockey Schools	Field Hockey Partic
Alabama	309	3,709	37	346		
Alaska	89	1,469	50	521		
Arizona	146	3,582	82	945		
Arkansas	395	5,900	33	165		
California	1,011	22,362	819	8,753	93	2,482
Colorado	258	9,030	117	1,755		
Connecticut	160	3,729	130	1,546	79	2,691
Delaware	37	860	16	191	35	1,119
D.C.	17	465	7	105		
Florida	394	6,905	259	2,337		
Georgia	327	9,006	135	1,408		
Hawaii	51	1,074	46	628		
Idaho	124	2,722	42	403		
Illinois	631	16,255	229	2,948	13	361
Indiana	395	10,000	185	18,000		
Iowa	491	14,146	185	1,571		
Kansas	366	7,678	180	1,032		
Kentucky	276	5,520	142	1,709		
Louisiana	366	8,052	52	624		
Maine	137	4,110	125	1,000	85	1,870
Maryland	153	3,783	114	1,300	108	3,282
Mass	310	9,145	216	2,395	204	7,118
Michigan	698	19,214	374	3,110	10	370
Minnesota	490	10,705	223	2,273		
Mississippi	264	4,336	20	154		
Missouri	528	13,603	143	1,640	30	921
Montana	182	4,059	53	595		
Nebraska	365	7,973	100	500		
Nevada	58	1,110	28	250		
N. Hamp.	83	2,600	40	900	55	1,200
N. Jersey	375	8,589	234	3,439	208	7,695
N. Mexico	122	2,711	55	588		
New York	711	17,557	401	5,316	265	9,158
N. Carolina	335	6,314	105	800		
N. Dakota	234	4,048	32	200		
Ohio	790	16,343	472	3,727	29	818
Oklahoma	489	10,210	91	708		
Oregon	247	6,175	182	2,730		
Penn	640	16,888	364	5,000	255	8,010
Rhode Is.	47	858	29	492	19	555
S. Carolina	209	4,693	34	269	1	49

GIRLS PARTICIPATION (con't)

STATE	Basketball Schools	Basketball Partic	Cross Country Schools	Cross Country Partic	Field Hockey Schools	Field Hockey Partic
S. Dakota	205	4,636	97	612		
Tennessee	352	9,912	121	847		
Texas	1,137	48,253	551	18,465		
Utah	90	1,803	54	527		
Vermont	46	1,083	27	273	33	1,121
Virginia	286	6,262	142	1,267	68	2,256
Washington	338	8,424	219	2,497		
W. Virginia	161	2,700	44	217		
Wisconsin	416	9,360	266	2,660		
Wyoming	73	1,600	20	250		

STATE	Golf Schools	Golf Partic	Gymnastics Schools	Gymnastics Partic	Soccer Schools	Soccer Partic
Alabama	16	68	18	180	9	169
Alaska			14	217	5	209
Arizona	24	112	25	348		
Arkansas	12	22	30	450		
California	48	288	227	4,991	251	6,395
Colorado			104	2,600	59	1,475
Connecticut			60	1,539	67	1,674
Delaware			5	63		
D.C.						
Florida	101	481	14	133	108	2,266
Georgia	26	58	40	719	57	991
Hawaii	13	50	3	25	35	619
Idaho	1	15				
Illinois	122	816	99	2,171	25	853
Indiana	130	1,300	147	2,700		
Iowa	338	3,261				
Kansas	37	332	28	323		
Kentucky	121	1,070	18	360	8	170
Louisiana	18	92	19	108	6	82
Maine	13	65	42	756	43	946
Maryland	45	52	46	709	44	1,086
Mass	41	73	102	1,722	128	4,305
Michigan	161	1,228	106	1,726	58	1,566
Minnesota	223	1,867	157	2,887	49	1,876
Mississippi	6	15			8	30
Missouri	56	510	18	360	43	1,169
Montana	44	527	20	304		
Nebraska	52	391	24	212		

GIRLS PARTICIPATION (con't)

STATE	Golf Schools	Golf Partic	Gymnastics Schools	Gymnastics Partic	Soccer Schools	Soccer Partic
Nevada	22	150				
N. Hamp.					20	400
N. Jersey	47	103	123	1,580	143	4,535
N. Mexico	32	119	17	163	14	376
New York	82	567	199	3,718	464	16,722
N. Carolina	6	50	4	59	21	500
N. Dakota	22	151	26	202		
Ohio	22	261	145	2,069	80	2,190
Oklahoma	75	675				
Oregon	68	408	58	870	60	1,500
Penn	174	1,930	100	1,990	47	1,128
Rhode Is.			28	387		
S. Carolina					4	74
S. Dakota	39	441	35	683		
Tennessee	49	98				
Texas	744	15,410				
Utah	49	947	34	614	7	35
Vermont	9	16	10	138	21	468
Virginia			119	1,508	54	1,577
Washington	72	389	73	1,612	92	2,539
W. Virginia	12	23	48	874		
Wisconsin	79	790	148	4,440		
Wyoming			12	100		

STATE	Softball fast Schools	Softball fast Partic	Softball slow Schools	Softball slow Partic	Swimming/ Diving Schools	Swimming/ Diving Partic
Alabama			114	1,789	13	130
Alaska					21	314
Arizona	104	3,087			17	250
Arkansas			15	225	17	255
California	919	22,840			443	12,715
Colorado					87	2,610
Connecticut	148	4,320			65	1,688
Delaware	33	816	2	48	16	379
D.C.					7	150
Florida			372	7,326	202	2,865
Georgia			165	3,470	47	563
Hawaii	49	805			34	409
Idaho						
Illinois	476	11,907			147	3,654

GIRLS PARTICIPATION (con't)

STATE	Softball fast Schools	Softball fast Partic	Softball slow Schools	Softball slow Partic	Swimming/Diving Schools	Swimming/Diving Partic
Indiana	82	1,900			163	3,500
Iowa	483	7,888			58	1,154
Kansas	28	852			33	796
Kentucky			87	1,914	25	285
Louisiana	41	5,240			27	280
Maine	132	2,376			30	450
Maryland	144	3,813			31	614
Mass	306	9,360			91	1,916
Michigan	592	15,551			203	4,673
Minnesota	253	7,134			120	3,040
Mississippi			68	1,214		
Missouri	278	5,719			49	1,359
Montana					15	169
Nebraska					32	610
Nevada	35	810			20	150
N. Hamp.	83	2,000				
N. Jersey	365	11,686			91	2,135
N. Mexico	39	767			22	332
New York	725	20,643			248	6,320
N. Carolina			326	6,950	40	569
N. Dakota						
Ohio	527	11,862			193	2,998
Oklahoma	210	3,150	108	1,620	41	492
Oregon	113	3,390			67	1,005
Penn	513	12,750			206	4,500
Rhode Is.			47	1,021		
S. Carolina	144	2,660				
S. Dakota						
Tennessee	181	3,449				
Texas					237	4,314
Utah					40	593
Vermont	45	1,259				
Virginia	192	3,929			41	905
Washington			202	5,137	94	2,194
W. Virginia					2	23
Wisconsin	240	6,000			110	3,850
Wyoming					25	300

GIRLS PARTICIPATION (con't)

STATE	Tennis Schools	Tennis Partic	Track/Field indoor Schools	Track/Field indoor Partic	Track/Field outdoor Schools	Track/Field outdoor Partic
Alabama	106	866	52	503	163	1,928
Alaska					36	567
Arizona	85	1,565			138	3,161
Arkansas	111	885			271	2,710
California	726	13,170			949	21,067
Colorado	101	1,878			246	9,840
Connecticut	117	2,452	25	596	143	4,290
Delaware	25	367	6	128	23	782
D.C.	11	110	7	140	10	200
Florida	285	2,462			328	6,386
Georgia	294	2,993			288	6,525
Hawaii	50	623			49	1,031
Idaho	39	568			123	2,389
Illinois	274	5,522	1	34	565	15,155
Indiana	264	4,500			378	10,700
Iowa	114	2,456			123	2,389
Kansas	113	1,654			373	8,036
Kentucky	177	1,529			192	3,140
Louisiana	130	780			32	6,440
Maine	60	540	35	420	111	2,442
Maryland	133	1,603	95	1,889	139	3,397
Mass	219	3,228	114	2,516	138	8,324
Michigan	300	4,841			612	17,928
Minnesota	170	3,292			425	9,242
Mississippi	99	698			183	2,574
Missouri	133	2,244			406	11,168
Montana	31	434			182	2,868
Nebraska	43	850			364	6,200
Nevada	22	200			52	1,000
N. Hamp.	33	330	15	300	40	1,200
N. Jersey	292	3,897	105	3,039	310	9,710
N. Mexico	44	487			117	1,857
New York	435	6,909	193	4,522	539	17,748
N. Carolina	208	2,638	27	221	226	5,934
N. Dakota	21	381			210	2,721
Ohio	355	4,961			723	20,333
Oklahoma	107	1,260			330	3,960

GIRLS PARTICIPATION (con't)

STATE	Tennis Schools	Tennis Partic	Track/Field indoor Schools	Track/Field indoor Partic	Track/Field outdoor Schools	Track/Field outdoor Partic
Oregon	115	920			241	7,230
Penn	333	4,990			452	13,500
Rhode Is.	31	526			28	869
S. Carolina	92	943			167	3,815
S. Dakota	17	237			202	4,136
Tennessee	193	3,474			184	5,704
Texas	1,039	15,922			1,117	44,910
Utah	56	606			97	2,097
Vermont	14	294	3	19	27	683
Virginia	199	2,367	86	1,666	263	7,091
Washington	210	3,346			307	7,162
W. Virginia	68	730			108	2,277
Wisconsin	160	3,200			389	11,070
Wyoming	11	75			73	1,000

STATE	Volleyball Schools	Volleyball Partic	Skiing downhill Schools	Skiing downhill Partic
Alabama	230	3,171		
Alaska	68	1,166		
Arizona	146	4,223		
Arkansas	79	950		
California	920	22,138	20	234
Colorado	253	6,325	7	84
Connecticut	113	2,384		
Delaware	21	513		
D.C.	12	180		
Florida	363	6,783		
Georgia	26	442		
Hawaii	55	1,037		
Idaho	120	2,848		
Illinois	638	17,385		
Indiana	395	9,800		
Iowa	334	1,908		
Kansas	357	8,266		
Kentucky	60	720		
Louisiana	177	2,024		
Maine			35	420
Maryland	137	3,022		
Mass	123	2,704	36	562
Michigan	606	16,423	71	749

GIRLS PARTICIPATION (con't)

STATE	Volleyball Schools	Volleyball Partic	Skiing downhill Schools	Skiing downhill Partic
Minnesota	488	13,215	42	494
Mississippi	22	294		
Missouri	370	9,428		
Montana				
Nebraska	364	8,900		
Nevada	56	950	12	150
N. Hamp.	18	200	32	400
N. Jersey	89	2,005	15	126
N. Mexico	111	2,661		
New York	650	16,414	67	982
N. Carolina	220	3,795		
N. Dakota	36	789	13	226
Ohio	748	8,423		
Oklahoma	176	2,112		
Oregon	248	4,960		
Penn	347	8,740		
Rhode Is.	34	763		
S. Carolina	143	2,067		
S. Dakota	47	1,203		
Tennessee	187	3,553		
Texas	795	37,225		
Utah	95	1,811		
Vermont			15	133
Virginia	114	1,992		
Washington	333	7,956		
W. Virginia	64	1,101		
Wisconsin	420	12,600		
Wyoming	71	1,450	7	75

MISC. SPORTS

SPORT	STATE	SCHOOLS	PARTIC
Archery	Alaska	1	8
	Arizona	11	112
	Illinois	1	20
	New York	11	117
Badminton	Arizona	34	541
	California	289	4,458
	Illinois	77	2,475
	Maryland	8	180

GIRLS PARTICIPATION
MISC. SPORTS (con't)

SPORT	STATE	SCHOOLS	PARTIC
	Massachusetts	1	13
	New York	61	934
Baseball	Alabama	1	9
	California	30	554
	Georgia	2	5
	Mississippi	1	4
	Nevada	1	4
	West Virginia	1	1
Bowling	Alabama	1	4
	Hawaii	30	309
	Illinois	100	1,540
	Iowa	30	466
	Michigan	18	228
	Nevada	14	170
	New Jersey	112	1,212
	New York	190	2,254
	Pennsylvania	57	550
	South Carolina	8	65
Canoeing (crew)	Hawaii	8	143
	Delaware	1	21
	West Virginia	1	10
Decathlon	Alabama	2	2
Fencing	Kentucky	7	56
	New Jersey	21	309
	New York	9	152
Ice Hockey	Massachusetts	10	48
Judo	Hawaii	1	7
Lacrosse	Delaware	5	187
	Maryland	35	1,579
	Massachusetts	18	734
	Michigan	1	30
	New Jersey	25	1,006
	New York	28	1,244
	Pennslyvania	49	1,585
Pentathlon	Alabama	3	6
	Arkansas	17	31
	Tennessee	21	23
Riflery	Alaska	10	66
	Georgia	12	39
	Hawaii	7	51
	Kentucky	17	17

MISC. SPORTS

	Massachusetts	3	17
	New York	16	77
	Pennsylvania	47	380
Skiing (cross-country)	Alaska	36	232
	Maine	65	252
	Minnesota	32	861
	New Hampshire	32	400
	Vermont	18	143
	Wyoming	7	90
Squash and Water Polo	California	17	651
	Florida	14	143
	Hawaii	3	14
	Illinois	2	29
	Nevada	1	15
	Pennsylvania	11	225
	Utah	4	60
Weightlifting and Wrestling	Florida	95	2,189
	Georgia	8	103
	California	1	6
	Vermont	1	2

INDIVIDUAL SPORTS OFFICIATING OPPORTUNITIES

CHAPTER VI

BASEBALL

Millions of people play baseball on the amateur, high school, collegiate, industrial, semi-professional and professional levels. Opportunities abound for qualified officials throughout the world because of this sport's international appeal.

Baseball, often called America's favorite pastime, began in the eastern United States in the mid-1800s. By 1876, the first professional major league, the National League, had been formed with the American League following in 1900.

Throughout the years the sport has spread to other countries and is now being played as an exhibition sport during the Summer Games of the Olympics. Baseball is now considered a major sport in Canada, Japan, Taiwan, the Netherlands, South Africa, Korea and many Latin American countries. It is played by organized teams for every age group from the eight-year olds in the Little League to the adults in the Old Timers League.

In the United States, professional baseball has become big business. It is estimated that every year approximately 30 million people purchase tickets to professional league games, while many more millions watch the games on television or listen to them on radio.

Organized baseball leagues are divided into three levels, amateur, minor and major leagues. There are three associations which govern amateur play for the younger players. They are the American Amateur Baseball Congress, Boys Baseball Inc. and the Little League Baseball Association. Local organizations such as park districts also have similar programs for youth. There are an estimated 7,000 Little League teams throughout the world. The National Baseball Congress sponsors amateur leagues for adults.

As of 1980, there were 13 minor leagues with a total of 110 teams. The leagues are divided into three classifications, Class AAA, Class AA and Class A. There is also a Rookie League which is not classified.

Most minor league teams play in the United States and some in Canada and Mexico.

The most well-known league is the major league which consists of the National League and the American League. Twelve professional teams play in the National League and 14 in the American League. Of the 26 teams playing, 24 are from cities in the United States and two are from Canada. There are approximately 1,040 professional baseball players (480 National and 560 American League), who play a regular season of 162 games between early April and late September or early October.

Each league holds a post-season playoff series to determine the league champions. The two league champions then play in the World Series, a best of seven games series for the World Championship. A special game is played during the regular season matching stars from both leagues against each other. This game is appropriately called the All-Star Game.

The number of umpires used per game varies on the different levels of play. A baseball game can be officiated by one umpire or six. The major leagues usually utilize four umpires per game. They are the *home plate umpire,* the *first base umpire,* the *second base umpire* and the *third base umpire.* Each umpire is responsible for calling the plays at his base. The home plate umpire has the additional responsibility of calling the pitches. The umpires on first and third bases call foul balls in their respective areas. The World Series and the All-Star Game utilize six umpires.

There is no other sport in the world where you will find more authorities than in the sport of baseball. Virtually everyone who knows anything about baseball claims to be an authority. This of course, causes a great deal of confusion and misunderstanding.

For the most part, however, the average spectator knows very little about the complexities of this national pastime. Baseball rules and regulations are very precise, and there are numerous conditional situations that dictate specific calls. For example, suppose a batted ball hits home plate and bounces outside the batter's box onto the field of play or suppose a ball is hit, spins upward and travels over foul territory but lands beyond the base in fair territory? Situations like this require a keen eye and a precise knowledge of the rules.

There are six basic situations that require the umpire to rule on a batted ball. These include 1) when the ball settles or is touched by a fielder before the batter and base runner reach first and third base, 2) when a hit ball passes over first or third base, 3) when the ball physically touches either first or third base after being hit, 4) when a fly ball first hits the ground beyond either first or third base, 5) when a fly ball is touched by a fielder and 6) when a fly ball is hit out of the playing field or park.

At the professional level, making the right call is very critical because the outcome of the game often hinges upon the narrow rulings called by a very astute official. More often than not, the spectators are unaware of conditional rulings, and a loud uproar ensues from fans and players alike.

Therefore, umpires must be highly qualified well before they ever enter professional baseball. They will have to have demonstrated an ability to consistently make accurate decisions in accordance with the established rules, and the players and spectators are allowed only the opportunity to shout their protests on deaf ears.

The possibility of making a mistake is extremely high, and every decision is closely scrutinized for flaws. If and when erratic or vacillating judgment is noticed, especially by the players, the game can quickly turn into a shouting match. This type of pressure often eliminates would-be sporting officials who have not made a conscientious effort to discipline themselves.

Most spectators believe that umpiring a baseball game is easy, and that they could perform the task if given the opportunity. This simply is not true. The average spectator could not last through the first inning, let alone nine innings of close calls, alert play and complex rule interpretation. The nature of the sport invites protests, arguments and disagreements from everyone. For instance, the average spectator is not aware that most officials carry a hand-held counter or indicator for recording balls and strikes. When a game has been interrupted for a prolonged period for any reason, and must resume, an official could look foolish if the count was not correct. Therefore, being prepared with a reliable counter or indicator is an important safeguard.

There is almost an endless array of special situations that command the attention of a qualified umpire. It is common knowledge among baseball enthusiasts that a batter gets a free ride to first base if hit by a pitcher's throw, but what if the batter fakes being hit? A batter is under an obligation to avoid being hit, and therefore any deliberate attempt to place himself in the direct path or any failure to move away from an obviously poor pitch could easily change an observant umpire's decision. The average spectator is not aware of these Catch-22 types of decisions that confront knowledgeable umpires.

In all, there are at least a dozen special situations that require a thorough knowledge of the rules and a keen umpire's eye to make an accurate call. They encompass everything from a batter stepping out of the batter's box before, during and after a pitch is thrown, to interference by the catcher. Tag situations have forever caused marginally qualified umpires a tremendous amount of grief and so have fumbled balls before and after a catch. When you add the possibility of two or more situations occurring simultaneously or in rapid succession, you begin to understand the need to acquire as much knowledge and experience as possible to qualify for major-league consideration.

As always, the best place to begin is at the amateur level. At this level a game will have either one or two officials. When there is only one official, little has to be cleared with team captains and coaches/managers prior to the start of the game. But in a two umpire game (or a game using more than two umpires), the umpires are under an obligation to coordinate their positions and plans in advance with the other officials. This means that well before the first ball is thrown, they must mutually decide which one will cover bases as players advance from one base to another. Also, it must be decided who calls fly out or trapped ball situations, or when a runner misses a base or whether a player technically dropped or caught the ball in a throwing situation.

It is an important pregame duty to establish each official's areas of responsibility. If coaches/managers or team captains are present, these decisions are also brought to their attention to avoid any misunderstanding during the game. In addition, any recently developed rulings or changes in game rules should be brought to the attention of both teams' coaches/managers and/or team captains.

It is also the umpire's duty to survey the playing field and any equipment for alterations or violations of game rules. All of the above duties must be completed prior to starting the game. Mind you, the foregoing involves merely the preliminary requirements before the game begins. As you can easily see, the game and subsequent rulings could become extremely complex and subject to question if you fail to agree upon who is covering what, when.

How to become a baseball official: The **first step** in the process is to contact your State High School Athletic Association or the National Federation of State High School Athletic Associations and request an application and an official rule book of regulations pertaining to baseball. At the same time, the **second step** is to request information pertaining to a listing of accredited local agencies or approved class training stations in your geographical area. You should make plans to attend the next open session. The **third step** is to study the materials so that you will be able to pass the written and practical examination. The **fourth step** is to apply for membership in one or more of the appropriate associations. This information can be obtained by asking your State High School Athletic Association, the Federation of State High School Athletic Associations or local agencies for their recommendations. See Appendix A, which is a listing of all state high school associations throughout the United States.

Applications take approximately two weeks to process. Fees will normally range between $10 and $20.

During this interim, contact your area recreational director(s) or junior high and high school baseball coach, and observe and/or volunteer to officiate with these types of community programs, or at the intramural level. Your involvement will provide you with invaluable practical experience.

NOTE: The chapter on "Getting Started" will provide you with the step-by-step procedure to progress from the amateur level to college level and professional level of sports officiatings.

You may also refer to Appendix E, which is a listing of private officiating schools and accredited college-level officiating courses throughout the United States. Also, in Appendix B you will find a listing of college conferences and other baseball associations throughout the United States.

Appendix C will provide you with professional associations that utilize the majority of professional officials.

Publications and periodicals are located in Appendix D. They will provide the serious individual with additional background and critical information on the sport.

The major manufacturers of sports-related equipment and supplies can be found in Appendix F. Each sport will require its officials to possess a proper uniform and other officiating equipment. These manufacturers can save you a tremendous amount of time and effort in locating exactly the right pieces of equipment.

COMPENSATION: At the recreational level or in intramural programs, salaries will range from $10 to $20 per game. Salaries for junior high school officials start at $17.50 to $27 per game (with two officials being used), and for high school junior varsity level the range is $20 to $34 per game and varsity level (using two officials) range from $21 to $45 for the umpire per game.

Salaries for college officials range from $50 to $60 per game plus travel and expenses. Statisticians, scorers and timers generally range from $20 to $30 per game.

Semi-professional baseball game umpires earn approximately $1,300 to $1,900 per month plus travel and per diem. The season spans from April to September of each year. In certain warmer climates, this season will be longer. There are 18 leagues at the semi-professional level. This includes Rookie Ball, Long A League, Class AA and Class AAA. **NOTE:** Major league umpires are usually selected from one of three professional baseball training camps: Joe Brinkman Umpiring School, Bill Kinnamon Umpires' School and Harry Wendelstedt Umpires' School.

For professional major league baseball officials (American League and National League), the yearly compensation ranges from $27,000 to $75,000 plus $97 daily for expenses. **NOTE:** Experienced umpires who are selected to handle the play-off games, the All-Star game and the World Series are compensated generously with the World Series' officials receiving approximately $15,000, the play-off officials receiving $14,000 and the All-Star Game officials receiving $2,500.

The Major League Umpire Association's strike during the 1984 season netted the sixty umpires a substantial increase in their compensation package. As a result of the strike, a pool has been established out of which the officials who work the World Series, Play-Off Series and the All-Star Game will be paid a cumulative sum of $225,000. The remaining funds are to be divided among all sixty umpires. Each umpire will receive an additional $3,000 in 1984, $4,000 in 1985 and $5,000 in 1986. Fringe benefits include complete medical coverage, pensions and travel accommodations.

GENERAL QUESTIONS PERTAINING TO BASEBALL

1. To start a baseball game you must have one or two umpires and two teams consisting of nine players each. (T) or (F)
2. The distance between home plate and first base is exactly 90 feet in regulation play. (T) or (F)
3. The pitcher stands sixty and 1/2 feet from home plate. (T) or (F)
4. When a player hits a ball thrown from the pitcher and the ball travels over the designated boundary or fence in fair play, this is considered a home-run. (T) or (F)
5. An official scorer must be designated by the home-team or officials before the start of the game. (T) or (F)
6. A bunted ball is considered a legal play if it stays in fair territory. (T) or (F)
7. If a pitcher hits the batter with a thrown ball, the batter is awarded advancement to first base. (T) or (F)
8. If a pitcher fakes a throw to first base while a runner is on first base, this is ruled a balk. (T) or (F)
9. It is illegal if the pitcher goes to his mouth while standing on the rubber (or pitcher's mound). (T) or (F)
10. If the ball rolls down the first base line and hits the base, that is located in foul and fair territory (both), the ruling is that the ball is fair. (T) or (F)
11. If the batter hits the ball out of the ball park in fair territory, but the ball hits an object and bounces back onto the playing field, the ruling is a homerun. (T) or (F)
12. If the batter hits the ball toward the fence and the outfielder jumps up and catches the ball, but on his way down, the ball leaves his glove and falls over the fence, the ruling is a four base error. (T) or (F)
13. If the pitcher throws a ball into the dirt and it gets past the catcher, the ruling is a wild pitch. (T) or (F)
14. The in-field fly rule is in effect when there are runners on first and second with one or no outs, and the batter pops up to the infield. (T) or (F)
15. If a batter hits the ball to left field and the left fielder throws his glove to stop or catch the ball, the officials will immediately rule an illegal play and determine the amount of bases to be awarded. (T) or (F)

Answers To Baseball Quiz

1. True
2. True
3. True
4. True
5. True
6. True
7. True
8. True
9. True
10. True
11. True
12. True
13. True
14. True
15. True

NATIONAL FEDERATION OF STATE HIGH SCHOOL ASSOCIATIONS BASEBALL OFFICIAL SIGNALS

A baseball official must know and be able to demonstrate the officially accepted signals. Each of the following drawings represents one specific signal that is utilized during an official game. Attempt to identify (name) the signal depicted in each drawing. Compare your answers to the correct answers located at the end of the chapter.

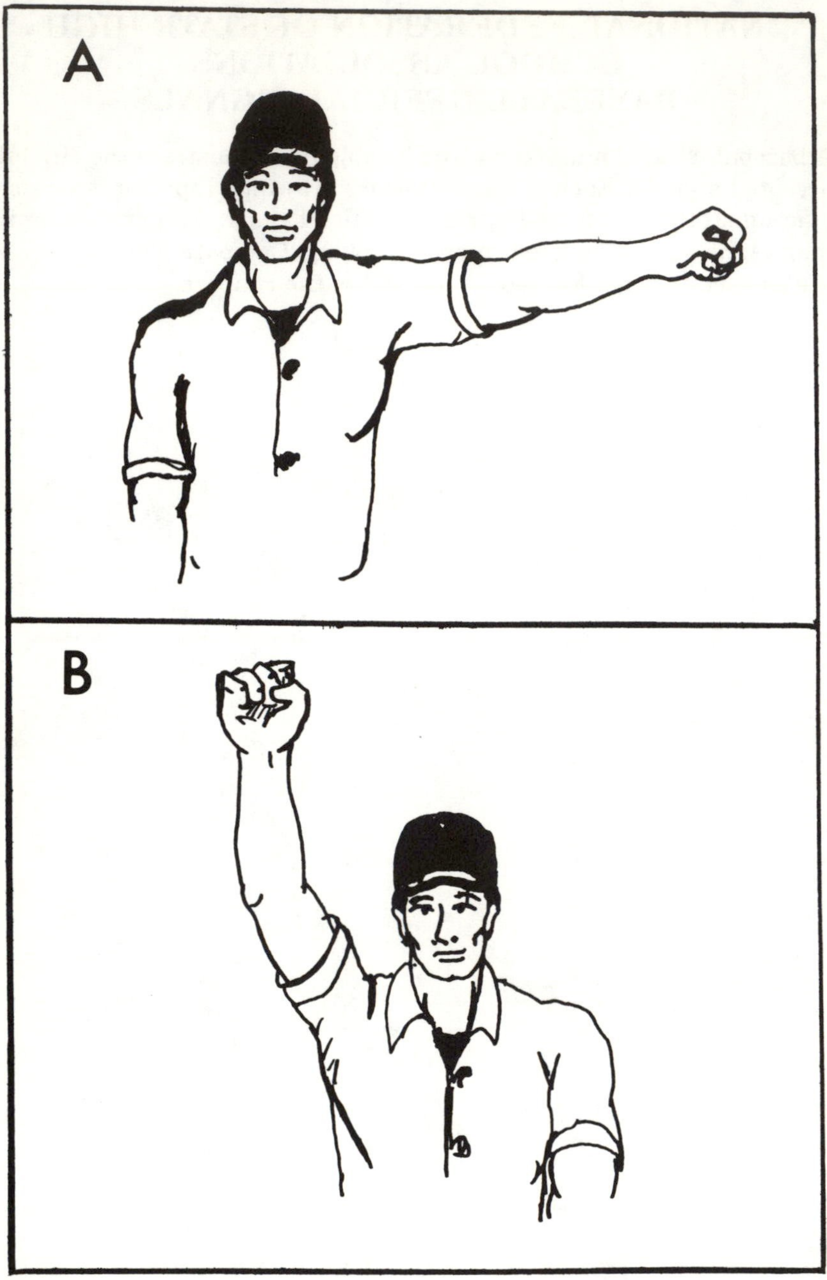
A
B

C

D

E

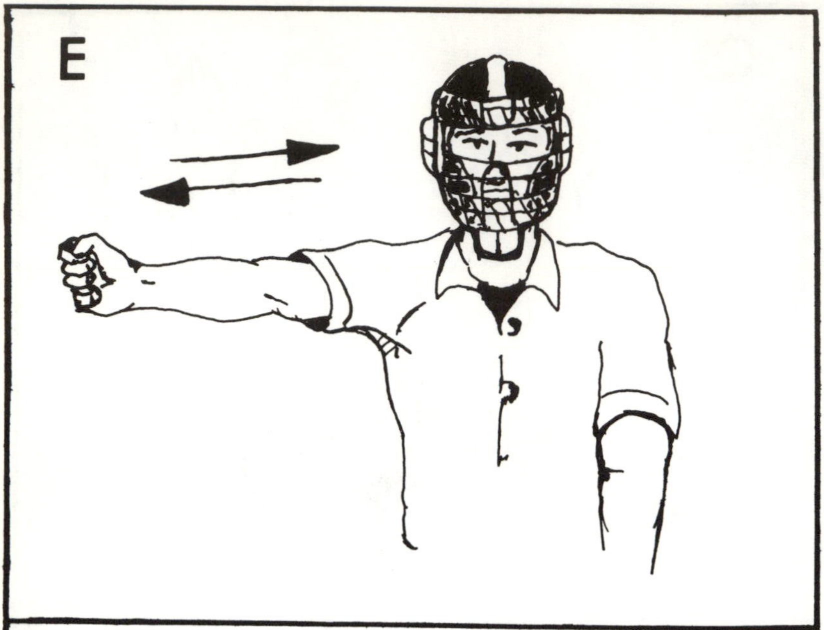

F

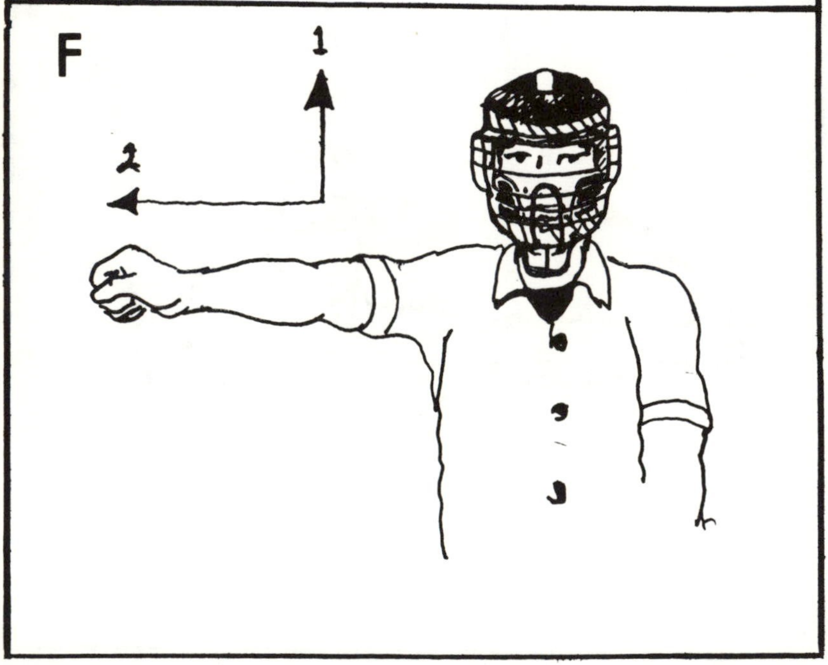

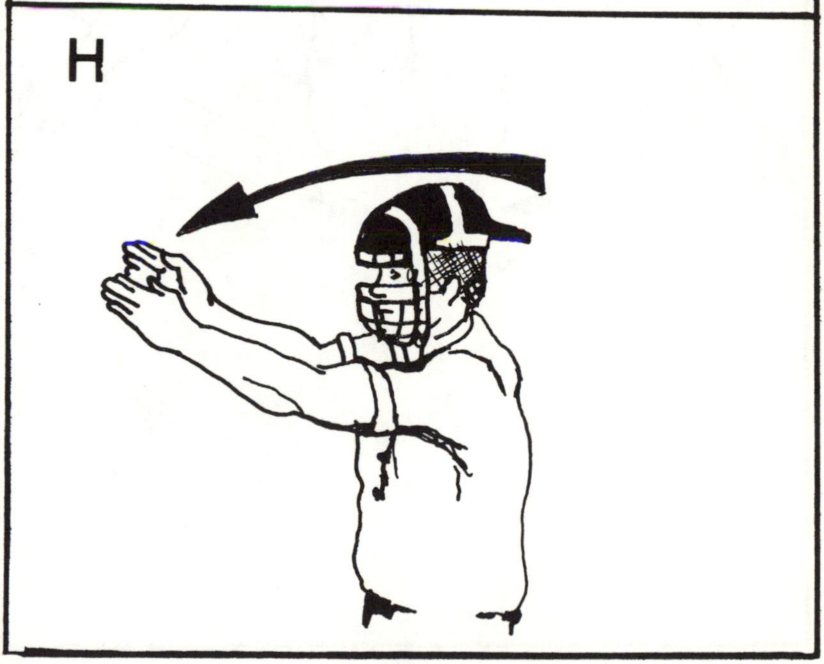

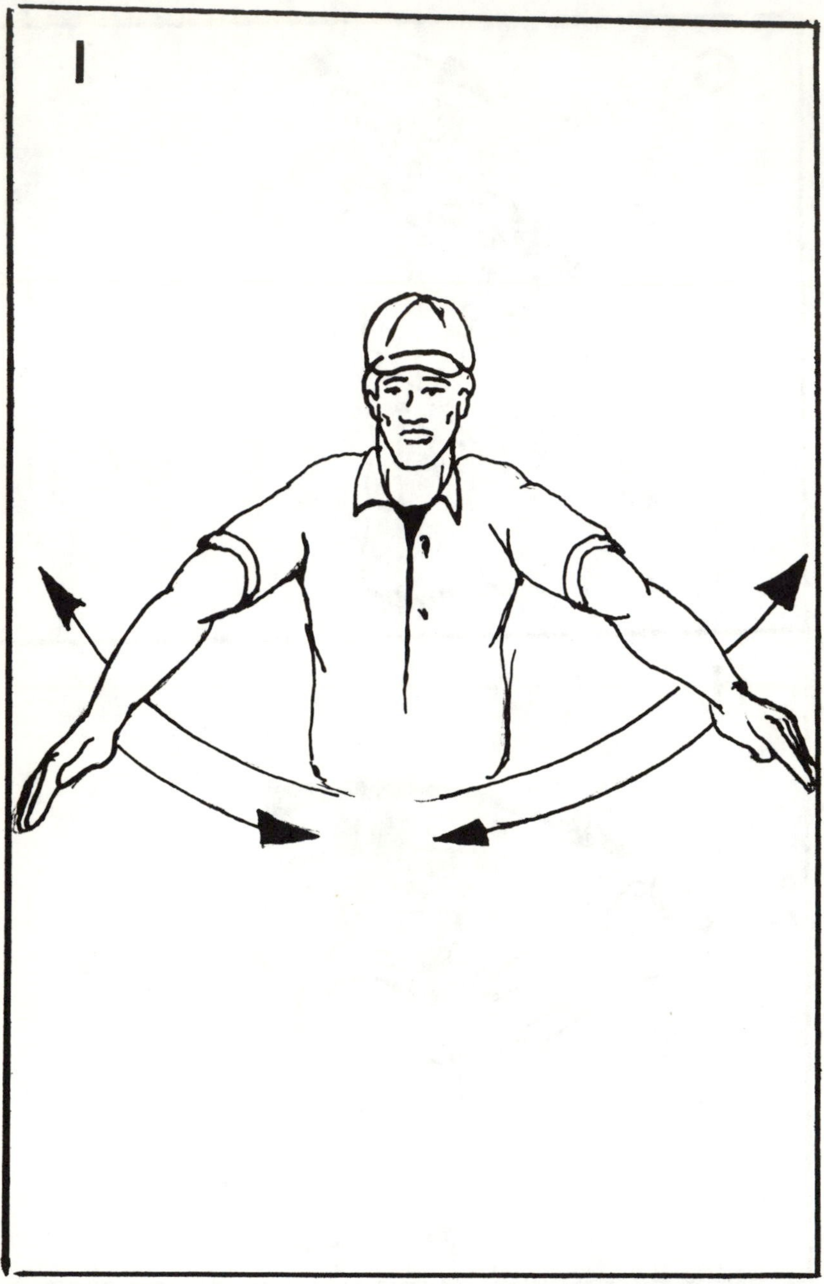
I

J

K

SIGNAL ANSWERS (Baseball):

A. Delayed Dead Ball as for Catcher Interference or illegal pitch followed by delivery of the ball to batter
B. Infield Fly
C. Ball Dead immediately as for batter being hit by pitch or batted ball touched by spectator
D. Fair or Foul Ball
E. Player is Out
F. Strike
G. Foul Tip
H. Foul Ball
I. Runner is Safe
J. Do Not Pitch and Time Out
K. Play Ball

CHAPTER VII

SOFTBALL

Softball is popular in United States, Canada and Japan. In the United States alone, more than 31 million people actively participate in the sport. There are approximately 175,000 plus teams competing in adult and Junior Olympics ASA softball activities as of 1984. The 1983-84 playing season was one of the most exciting periods on record. There were more games, more championships and special events than ever before. These included such events as: the Pan-American Games, the National Sports Festival, the National All-Star Series, the Hall of Fame Classic and the ASA National Championships.

Softball is especially popular in schools, recreational and industrial programs because it can be played on a smaller field than baseball, and does not require as much equipment. The game, which originated in Chicago, was developed by George W. Hancock in 1887 as an indoor game. It was adapted for outdoor play in 1895 by Lewis Rober of the Minneapolis Fire Department, and the game as it is played today more closely resembles Rober's version.

Until the 1930s, the game was played by ten different sets of rules. In 1933, the Amateur Softball Association of America (ASA) was established to govern and promote softball in the United States. The association set up a committee which established the set of rules now used by teams throughout the world.

The International Softball Federation was formed in 1952 and governs all international competition. There are 50 member federations and their teams compete in annual, regional, national and international tournaments.

The primary differences between baseball and softball are: that the bases are closer together in softball, the softball pitcher stands closer to home plate than in baseball, the base runners cannot leave a base until after the ball is pitched, all softball pitches are delivered underhanded, and a regulation softball game is only seven innings.

The game of softball is divided into two types, slow-pitch and fast-pitch. Slow-pitch makes up over 80% of all softball competition. There are ten players on each slow-pitch team and nine players on fast-pitch teams.

The game of softball, like baseball, is officiated by one or more umpires. In a one-umpire situation, the umpire stands behind home plate. In a multiple umpire situation, the other umpires are stationed at each base and are responsible for calling plays at their respective bases.

Softball is rapidly expanding, and with 195,000 organized teams currently playing, there are numerous opportunities for umpires in amateur softball.

How to become a softball official: The **first step** is to join the Amateur Softball Association of America (ASA), 2801 Northeast 50th Street, Oklahoma City, Oklahoma 73111. (405) 424-5266. The **second step** in the process is to check with your state high school athletic association for the name and address of your area ASA representative. You must be certified by ASA and your state high school athletic association before you can qualify for structured compensation. The **third step** is to contact your State High School Athletic Association or the National Federation of State High School Athletic Associations and request an application and official rule book of regulations pertaining to softball. At the same time request information pertaining to a listing of accredited and approved training courses in your geographical area. You should make plans to attend the next open session. The **fourth step** is to study the material so that you will be able to pass the written and practical examination. The **fifth step** is to apply for membership in one or more of the appropriate associations. The necessary information can be obtained by asking your State High School Athletic Association, the Federation of State High School Athletic Associations or local agencies for their recommendations. See Appendix A, which is a listing of all the state high school athletic associations throughout the United States.

Applications take approximately two weeks to process. Fees will normally range between $10 and $20.

During this interim, contact your area recreational director(s), junior high school softball coaches, and observe and/or volunteer to officiate with these types of community programs, or at the intramural level. Your involvement will provide you with invaluable practical experience.

NOTE: The Chapter on "Getting Started" will provide you with the step-by-step procedure to progress from the amateur level to college level and professional level of sports officiatings.

You may also refer to Appendix E, which is a listing of private officiating schools and accredited college-level officiating courses throughout the United States. Also, in Appendix B you will find a listing of college conferences and other softball associations throughout the United States.

Appendix C will provide you with professional associations that utilize the majority of professional officials.

Publications and periodicals are located in Appendix D. They will provide the serious individual with additional background and critical information on the sport.

The major manufacturers of sports-related equipment and supplies can be found in Appendix F. Each sport will require its officials to possess a proper uniform and other officiating equipment. These manufacturers can save you a tremendous amount of time and effort in locating exactly the right pieces of equipment.

COMPENSATION: Officials are compensated at the recreational level: $14 to $18 per game. At the junior high (girls), $15 to $27 per game using one official. At the high school level salaries range from $18 to $34 per game. Varsity competition, salaries range from $20 to $45 per game.

Women's championship games (college level) using three officials are $35 plus travel and per diem.

Information pertaining to officiating at the professional softball level can be obtained directly by contacting the Amateur Softball Association (ASA), 2801 Northeast 50th Street, Oklahoma City, OK 73111, or call: (405) 424-5266, or contact the National Federation of State High School Athletic Associations, 11724 Plaza Circle, Box 20626, Kansas City, MO 64195, or call: (816) 464-5400.

Umpire's Examination (Softball):

The following sample test consists of 25 basic questions. A similar test consisting of approximately 105 questions would be administered to those individuals desiring to become registered umpires. The questions are generally based upon the information found in the official rule book published and distributed by the National Federation.

Questions require either a true/false or multiple choice response. A current test (similar to the one outlined below) is administered at a local or regional facility, and can be given by a State ASA Commissioner, local umpires association, local recreation department or military officer responsible for overseeing sports activities.

SAMPLE UMPIRE TEST

FIELD

1. Home plate is 17 inches wide and includes the black safety rim that is around it. (T-F)
2. For purposes of the game, the eight foot radius around the pitcher's plate exists even if the ground crew does not chalk in a visible line. (T-F)

DEFINITIONS

3. It is not a charged conference when the team representative enters the field from the dugout and removes the pitcher from the pitching position, provided the individual advises the plate umpire prior to crossing a foul line. (T-F)
4. Obstruction and interference do not require physical contact to be penalized. (T-F)

EQUIPMENT

5. A bat ring type weight which comes off a bat while a batter is warming up is dangerous equipment and must be removed from the playing field. (T-F)
6. A bat which has a new coat of paint identical to the original may be used in the game. (T-F)

PLAYERS & SUBSTITUTES

7. A violation of the re-entry rule results in the use of an ineligible player and a forfeit if a protest is lodged by the offended team during the game. (T-F)
8. After the line-up card has been turned into the umpire and to the official scorer, changes may be made in the batting order without it being considered a substitution until game time. (T-F)

THE GAME

9. A protest can be made in certain cases on an umpire's judgment call. (T-F)
10. A regulation game may have less than five innings completed. (T-F)

FAST PITCHING

11. The pitcher may pitch the first two pitches to a batter using a windmill delivery and switch to the sling shot delivery for the next pitch. (T-F)
12. In Fast Pitch, an illegal pitch is ignored if the batter hits the pitch and reaches first base safely, and all baserunners advance at least one base. (T-F)

SLOW PITCHING

13. The pitcher may have one or both feet in contact with the pitching plate prior to delivering the ball to the plate. (T-F)
14. A pitch that is not hit may be called a strike when the runner leaves the base too soon. (T-F)

BATTING

15. If the batter drops the bat and it rolls into the batted ball in fair territory, it is a dead ball and the batter is out. (T-F)
16. The award of two bases for an overthrow for the batter is always made starting from home plate. (T-F)
17. When a defensive player has the ball and is waiting to tag the runner, the runner may attempt to return to the previous base. (T-F)

MECHANICS

18. An umpire should not describe pitches that are balls by calling ball inside, ball a little deep, or ball too high. (T-F)
19. Short bibbed umpire caps are recommended on the bases or when a mask is not being used behind the home plate. (T-F)

POSITIONING QUESTIONS

20. (FP Two umpire system) With runners on first base and second base, the approximate starting position of the umpire is (a) Outside the foul line, left and behind first base, (b) Behind the base line between the short stop and third-base man, (c) Right and behind third base, (d) Left field, outside the base line between first and second base.
21. (FP or SP Three umpire system) With no runners on and a fly to center field the first base umpire should rotate to ________ position to wait for the next play.

TAG-UPS

22. (FP or SP Two umpire system) On a fly ball near the out of play line in the right field area, the base umpire may need to help on tag-up appeals at any base. (T-F)
23. (FP or SP Three umpire system) Runners on first and second base, the first base umpire has the batter runner tagging first base. (T-F)

RULE CHANGES

24. The traditional "donut ring" is no longer allowed on a bat used to warm-up by the on-deck batter. (T-F)
25. If a batter is hit by an illegal pitch, he is awarded first base and all runners are awarded one base. (T-F)

As you can see from this sample softball umpire's examination, some degree of conscientious study is required to successfully complete the test.

Answers To Softball Quiz

1. True
2. False
3. True
4. True
5. True
6. False
7. True
8. False
9. False
10. False
11. False
12. True
13. False
14. False
15. False
16. False
17. True
18. False
19. True
20. (a)
21. Mound
22. False
23. True
24. False
25. False

CHAPTER VIII

BASKETBALL

Basketball has the distinction of holding more spectator attention than any other sport. Annually viewed by more than 100 million spectators during a season that runs from October to June, the game is played by more than 40 million people throughout the United States and millions more around the world.

Since its invention in 1891, basketball has grown and is now considered a major amateur, high school, college and professional sport. It is a sport played equally by men and women. There are more than 20,000 high school boys teams and 18,000 high school girls teams throughout the United States. On the collegiate level more than 1,200 colleges and universities have basketball teams. It is estimated that over 34 million people view college basketball games each year. Most of these teams belong to one of more than 100 college conferences.

Women's collegiate basketball is supervised and governed by the Association for Intercollegiate Athletics for Women (AIAW), which has approximately 900 members.

Although professional teams were formed a few years after the invention of the game, professional basketball did not gain popularity until the late 1940s. Professional basketball became organized on a national level in 1946. The National Basketball Association (NBA) is comprised of 18 teams which play an 82-game season, along with a playoff series, World Championship and an All-Star Game. There are 276 NBA players in the league as of 1984.

The game is played by teams of five and is, on most levels, officiated by two officials. The referee is the chief official, but the umpire also calls fouls and violations. Some games utilize three officials.

Scorers and timers assist the officials. In professional and women collegiate basketball games one scorer and two timers are used. One of the timers operates the shot clock.

Few sports are more demanding upon officials than basketball. Here, the sports official must be in as good physical shape as the players, as it is an activity that demands continuous positioning and repositioning to monitor court mechanics.

The National Organization of Commissioners has developed a uniform guide of rules and court play. Most organized conferences have adopted these rules, and thus game play is well standardized throughout the country.

As in baseball and football, officiating basketball as a professional requires practical experience over a period of time to develop judgment, accurate timing and ideal positioning.

Unlike amateur baseball, organized basketball usually has more than one official because it has been shown to be nearly impossible to physically perform the duties accurately using one official. Fast breaking play has all but eliminated the one sports official from serious consideration. Therefore, the overview of duties applies to a multiple staff of officials.

PRE-GAME DUTIES:

Referee — Pre-Game: With more officials participating in the decision-making process, the interpersonal relationships that must be developed and maintained are more complex, and thus more demanding. The amount of time required to successfully perform pregame activities is greater than for baseball. In general, officials' responsibilities fall into four categories which consist of 1) the officials' pregame conference, 2) inspection of equipment and court for condition and legal play, 3) review of instructions with timekeepers and scorers (two factors that are more critical to the game than perhaps to baseball which is governed in time length by the number of innings), and 4) pregame meeting with coaches and captains from both teams. Nothing will contribute to a poorly officiated event more than the failure of officials to hold a well planned pregame conference. The better the communications and understanding among the officials prior to the game, the better the game will proceed on course and on schedule.

Another important consideration for holding pregame conferences among officials is to anticipate unruly behavior among members of either team, the spectators and in some cases, a combination of both. Rivalry between schools, cities and teams should be anticipated, and a pregame conference is an excellent way to reduce otherwise uncontrollable demonstrations or perhaps altercations.

Teams have been known to test officials for courage and technical knowledge. Some have resorted to employing clever tactics and then challenging the official's every call or pretending to be totally surprised when caught committing an otherwise obvious foul. Such tactics are common to the game. New officials are often intimidated. When this occurs, the players begin to take hold of the game in an attempt to badger their opponents. For this reason, it is very important for officials to be prepared to take charge and demonstrate their ability to do so. Strategy that has been carefully laid out prior to the start of the game in anticipation of an incident will go a long way toward preventing one from developing.

INSPECTING FACILITIES & EQUIPMENT: This sport has a specific rule which requires the game officials to inspect the game facilities and equipment prior to the start of each game. This inspection includes the basketball, the baskets, backboards and the floor markings. The purpose of the inspection is to detect alterations or modifications which do not meet regulation specifications. An official who fails to properly inspect for alterations or unauthorized modifications is in dereliction of duty.

Floor markings constitute a major aspect of the game. Floors with numerous or worn out markings should be inspected with additional care and boundaries should be carefully marked to avoid confusion and delay in the game.

Novice officials should seriously consider a check list pad with prerecorded items scheduled for inspection. Once a routine has been developed, inspection time can be reduced. In the long run, potential trouble situations can be eliminated and valuable time and energy saved.

SCORERS AND TIMEKEEPERS: During the pregame conference, the official should designate an individual to be the official scorer. It is the official's duty to advise the scorer of the methods or procedures to be utilized throughout the game including the procedure for designating players who have committed a foul, the time requirements for sending in substitutes, and the method for signalling an official. The scorer is responsible for properly noting the score and the personal fouls committed and by whom. The scorer has a duty to double check each entry that will become an official record.

When an electronic scoreboard is being used, scores should be regularly checked against the running score totals. Defective or malfunctioning equipment can rarely be corrected during the process of the game.

Timekeepers must also be properly instructed similar to scorekeepers. It is the timekeepers who will officially end each period, and thus their performance can have a tremendous influence upon the outcome of the game, especially when the score is close.

Once the official clock, watch or timepiece has been designated, only this instrument is to be used. This is critical because there can be no questions raised about "my clock and his watch" agreement. Each timepiece may differ slightly, but once the official timepiece has been selected, potential disputes can be eliminated.

When there are two timekeepers, each is responsible for watching the other's performance and sharing in the responsibility of indicating the end of each period. For example, if one timekeeper is making the last ten second count-down while watching the clock or timer, the other should hold the signaling device while watching the court action. This is probably the only safe way to proceed if time is called during the final critical seconds in a close game. When the game is resumed, the count can be started accurately at the point that it was interrupted.

In the event a signaling device fails to properly announce the ending of a period, or perhaps it could not be heard, it is the timekeeper's responsibility to immediately notify the official. Naturally, a score that changed during the interim or a foul committed will have to be decided upon by the official. In some cases, the final decision will be made by the timekeeper if the referee is without the necessary knowledge which would alter a ruling.

How to become a basketball official: The **first step** in the process is to contact your State High School Athletic Association or the National Federation of State High School Athletic Associations and request an application and official rule book of regulations pertaining to basketball. At the same time, the **second step** is to request information pertaining to a listing of accredited local agencies or approved class training stations in your geographical area. You should make plans to attend the next open session. The **third step** is to study the materials so that you will be able to pass the written and practical examination. The **fourth step** is to apply for membership in one or more of the appropriate associations. The necessary information can be obtained by asking your State High School Athletic Association, the Federation of State High School Athletic Associations or local agencies for their recommendations. See Appendix A, which is a listing of all the state high school associations throughout the United States.

Applications take approximately two weeks to process. Fees normally range between $10 and $20.

During this interim, contact your area recreational director(s), your junior high and high school basketball coach, and observe and/or volunteer to officiate with these types of community programs, or at the intramural level. Your involvement will provide you with invaluable practical experience.

NOTE: The Chapter on "Getting Started" will provide you with the step-by-step procedure to progress from the amateur level to the college level and professional level of sports officiatings.

You may also refer to Appendix E, which is a listing of private officiating schools and accredited college-level officiating courses throughout the United States. Also, in Appendix B you will find a listing of college conferences and other basketball associations throughout the United States.

Appendix C will provide you with professional associations that utilize the majority of professional officials.

Publications and periodicals are located in Appendix D. They will provide the serious individual with additional background and critical information on the sport.

The major manufacturers of sports-related equipment and supplies can be found in Appendix F. Each sport will require its officials to possess a proper uniform and other officiating equipment. These manufacturers can save you a tremendous amount of time and effort in locating exactly the right pieces of equipment.

COMPENSATION: At the recreational level or intramural programs, salaries range from $10 to $20 per game. Salaries for junior high school officials start at $17.50 to $30 per official (with two officials being used), and for high school junior varsity level the range is $20 to $38 per official and varsity level (using two officials) ranges from $35 to $50 for the referee per game. When a high school game of basketball is locally televised, officials' fee compensation is typically as follows: Play-by-play announcer $150, color commentator $100, statistician $50, game statistician and security $22 each, and ball boy $9.

Members of the Amateur Basketball Association of the United States earn from $25 to $150 per game depending upon experience and level of competition.

Salaries for college officials range from $150 to $300 per game depending upon experience, knowledge and rate standing, plus 50 cents per mile when the event is more than 200 miles away, and per diem expenses. Statisticians, scorers and timers generally range from $20 to $30 per game.

According to information from the Collegiate Commissioners Association of Basketball Supervisors of the 12 major Division I Conferences, the Big Ten pays a top fee of $300 to referees who work regular season games, the SEC and ACC Conferences pay $250, PAC-10 pays $225 per game, the Big Eight (Mid-American, PCAA, SWC and WAC) pays $200 per game, Missouri Valley Conference pays $185 per game, and the ECAC (Southern) pays $150 per game. Ten of the 12 leagues utilize three-man crews for their conference games, with the ECAC and the Mid-American Conference as exceptions. Travel expenses tend to vary greatly, with most assuming the tab for air travel.

For NCAA play offs, Divisions I, II and III, each man receives a minimum of $150 to $400 per game depending upon experience. NOTE: For play offs and conference tournaments, each official's fee will be raised $50 higher.

Semi-professional basketball games (NBA Pro-Am Leagues) rookies start at approximately $20 to $40 per game. The NBA uses 29 officials per season and CBA uses 30 officials. The Pro-Am League has teams in 17 cities throughout the country, and each city uses approximately 20 officials. Officials in the Pro-Am are considered interns. The NBA uses an official development program which utilizes a "step ladder" system for officials. These officials will start at the Pro-Am level and work that circuit for two or three years. From here they proceed to the Continental Basketball Association (CBA) where they can be assigned approximately 31 games per season, usually for one year or perhaps two years. At this level, compensation is $90 per game during the first year and $100 per game for the second year season. If the official is there for a third year, the rate is $115 per game. The next level is 62 games in the NBA. A full time NBA official will officiate 82 games.

At the professional level (NBA), for minor officials such as timekeepers, scorers and statisticians, fees range from $35 to $100. Major NBA officials receive anywhere from $350 to $1,500 per game. It should be understood that these officials have acquired a wealth of knowledge, practical experience plus the necessary rating and recommendations. NBA play-offs range from $800 to $1,500 per game plus travel.

For professional basketball officials, the yearly compensation can easily range from $30,000 to $100,000. NOTE: First-year "rookies" serving with a three-year contract, receive $28,000 to $40,000 a year. Officials with 15 or more years of service receive $85,000 to $90,000 on a three-year contract. After 19 years, salaries can reach $115,000 plus.

GENERAL QUESTIONS PERTAINING TO BASKETBALL

1. A field goal is counted as two or three points. (T) or (F)
2. A foul shot will count as one point. (T) or (F)
3. To start a game, each side must have five players. (T) or (F)
4. A held ball occurs when opponents have their hands so firmly on the ball that control cannot be obtained without undue roughness. (T) or (F)
5. Holding is personal contact with an opponent which interferes with another player's freedom or movement. (T) or (F)
6. A multiple throw is a succession of free throws attempted by the same team. (T) or (F)
7. A pass is movement of the ball caused by a player who throws, bats or rolls the ball to another player. (T) or (F)
8. Dunking or stuffing a basketball is legal. (T) or (F)
9. Extra period is the extension of playing time necessary to break a tie score. (T) or (F)
10. A foul is an infraction of the rules which is chargeable and penalized against the offender. (T) or (F)
11. Members of the same squad shall not wear identical numbers. (T) or (F)
12. Blocking is illegal personal contact with impedes the progress of an opponent. (T) or (F)
13. A bonus free throw is a second free throw which is awarded for each common foul (except a player control foul) committed by a player. (T) or (F)
14. Basket interference occurs when a player touches the ball or any part of the basket while the ball is on or within the basket. (T) or (F)
15. Boundary lines of the court consist of "end" and "sidelines". (T) or (F)

Answers To Basketball Quiz

1. True
2. True
3. True
4. True
5. True
6. True
7. True
8. True
9. True
10. True
11. True
12. True
13. True
14. True
15. True

NATIONAL FEDERATION OF STATE HIGH SCHOOL ASSOCIATIONS BASKETBALL OFFICIAL SIGNALS

A basketball official must know and be able to demonstrate the officially accepted signals. Each of the following drawings represents one specific signal that is utilized during an official game. Attempt to identify (name) the signal depicted in each drawing. Compare your answers to the correct answers located at the end of the chapter.

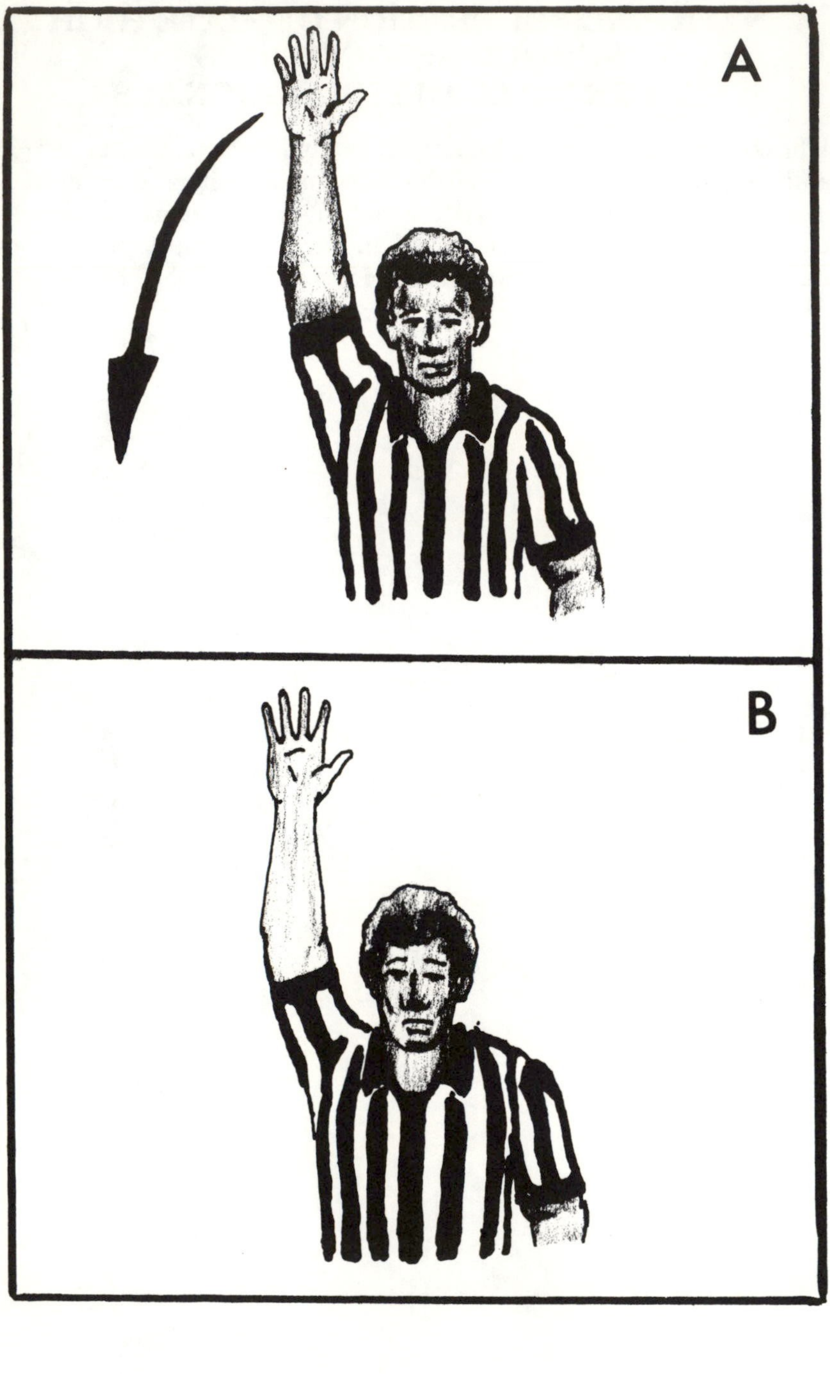
A
B

C

D

E

F

G
H

I
J

K

L

M
N

O

P

Q

R

S

T

U

V

W

X

Y

SIGNAL ANSWERS (Basketball):

A. Start Clock
B. Stop Clock or do not start clock
C. Stop Clock for Foul
D. Technical Foul
E. Holding
F. Blocking
G. Pushing or Charging
H. Illegal use of hands
I. Becking Substitute, ball dead -Clock Stopped
J. Stop Clock for Jump Ball
K. Illegal Dribble
L. Three Second Violation
M. Player Control Foul
N. Traveling
O. Over and Back or Carrying the Ball
P. Throw-in, Free Throw or Designated Spot Violation
Q. 5 or 10 second violation (use both hands for 10)
R. Direction Signal
S. No Score
T. Goal Counts or is Awarded
U. Point(s) scored (use 1 or 2 fingers)
V. Direction Signal
W & X. Lack of Action Count with visible wrist flick (Point toward team responsible)
Y. Bonus Free Throw (for second throw drop one arm — for two throw use one arm with two fingers)

CHAPTER IX

FOOTBALL

Football, a game originally developed from Rugby and Soccer, has more television spectators than any other sport viewed on the screen. Annually watched by more than 200 million spectators in United States, Canada and Japan during seasons that run from August through January (except USFL which runs from February to July), the game is played by more than 35 million people throughout the United States. Since 1869, football has played a major role at the amateur, high school, college and professional levels.

As of 1980, there were more than 600 colleges and universities with football teams which belonged to one of the 60 college conferences. These conferences set up the standards for competition. All college football teams belong to one of three intercollegiate athletic organizations, the National Collegiate Athletic Association (NCAA), the College Football Association (CFA) or the National Association of Intercollegiate Athletics (NAIA).

Professional football, as we now know it, began in 1970 with the merging of the American Football League (AFL) and the National Football League (NFL). The NFL is comprised of a total of 28 teams with a total of 1,372 players. The teams are divided into two conferences, the American Football Conference (AFC) and the National Football Conference (NFC). Each conference has 14 teams. The teams play a regular season of 16 games and depending on their season record they may advance to the playoff series and ultimately the Superbowl.

In 1981 the United States Football League was formed. The new league's season runs from February to July, but this is expected to change by 1986 in order to become more competitive with the NFL. Because of the extremely large salaries available in the USFL several players have switched leagues. Officials are also switching although the compensation is not as generous as in the NFL.

If there was ever any other sport next to gladiators charging into each other that has caused more spectator excitement, it has to be the game of football. More injuries are recorded in football than in any other contact sport. By the very nature of the game, it attracts individuals who are out to prove themselves and win either acceptance or respect among their peers, opponents and fans alike. With the help of radio and television, football has become a multi-billion dollar industry, and officials share in the financial rewards generated through their participation.

The game may be free-wheeling to the spectators and fans, but it is tightly controlled through strict application of guidelines, rules and regulations. The game of football, on the professional level, is officiated by a crew of seven officials, although the game can be officiated with any number of officials from four to seven.

The *referee* is the chief official and has ultimate control of the game. He is assisted by the *umpire,* who stands behind the defensive line and watches for fouls. The *head linesman* stands at the end of the line of scrimmage and supervises the marking crew and marks forward progress of the ball. The *field judge* stands opposite the head linesman and times the game.

Collegiate football games have six officials, the four listed above and the following: a *back judge* who assists the other officials when the play progresses down field (in professional football, the back judge stands 15 feet behind the offensive team and watches for fouls), and an alternate. Professional games also utilize a *line judge* who helps watch for fouls on the line. All football officials hold concurrent jurisdiction although each official is designated specific responsibilities.

Professional football officials have generally demonstrated an ability to coordinate and divide their respective field responsibilities. There is a wide range of equipment that must be properly maintained and regularly inspected. Pregame conferences are generally used to review any special arrangements and make specific assignments. And because each official holds specific areas of responsibility, there are generally few disputes that arise among football officials.

The two most important elements of the game center on the quality of the playing field itself, including how well it is marked or layed-out, and the football's physical condition. Usually, there is a dual inspection of the ball to ensure that it meets official standards; one is performed by the referee who will turn it over to the field judge for final inspection. Similarly, the playing field will be inspected by at least two of the officials. This double inspection procedure ensures proper conditions or at least reduces the possibility of embarrassing errors or problems that could develop during or after the game.

Naturally, the quality and condition of the field is an important factor, for a missing line or an altered end zone line can seriously affect accurate decisions. In a game that is played in terms of gained inches, feet and yards, proper care must be taken to ensure that markings are accurate and visible. Serious conditions must be corrected before the start of the game.

The umpire is required by game rules to inspect the players' equipment, primarily because of the extensive amount of bodily contact involved. This is not an optional rule, but a mandatory one. Even bandages and padding are subject to this type of personal and physical inspection.

The head linesman requires the assistance of three people, one to place the down marker and the other two to hold the chain marker at each end. Instruction to each assistant is very important. Emphasis should be placed upon the importance of not making any change or movement without specific instruction from the head linesman; otherwise confusion could easily result. For example, in the event of a penalty being called, moving the yard marker prematurely would cause a great many problems if the ball had to be brought back and played over.

Specific instructions from the head linesman to assistant linesman holding the down marker include: 1) placement should be made at the forward point of the ball as directed, 2) the stake should be turned to indicate the proper down (i.e., 1st, 2nd, 3rd or 4th), 3) movement should not be made until assistants are specifically directed to do so.

Specific instructions from the head linesman to the assistants holding the chain include: 1) placement should be made so that the home team's assistant is holding that end of the chain being defended by his team and the other chainman of course is responsible for the opposite end, 2) like the down marksman, the chain should not be moved until such directions are given, 3) in order to minimize injury, when plays are made too close to the sidelines, the chainman nearest the play should move his stake away from the sidelines. If the other end is accurately held in place, positioning will not be affected.

The field judge is responsible for keeping time on the field. He is responsible for overseeing those who operate electronic timing devices if the facility supports such equipment. To assure that he knows when to start or stop the clock, the field judge will indicate that fact with the proper hand signals.

How to become a football official: The **first step** in the process is to contact your State High School Athletic Association or the National Federation of State High School Athletic Associations and request an application and official rule book of regulations pertaining to football. At the same time, the **second step** is to request information pertaining to a listing of accredited local agencies or approved class training stations in your geographical area. You should make plans to attend the next open session. The **third step** is to study the materials so that you will be able to pass the written and practical examination. The **fourth step** is to apply for membership in one or more of the appropriate associations. The necessary information can be obtained by asking your State High School Athletic Associations, the Federation of State High School Athletic Associations or local agencies for their recommendations. See Appendix A, which is a listing of all the state high school associations throughout the United States.

Applications take approximately two weeks to process. Fees will normally range between $10 and $20.

During this interim, contact your area recreational director(s), your junior high and high school football coach, and volunteer to observe and/or officiate with these types of community programs, or at the intramural level. Your involvement will provide you with invaluable practical experience.

NOTE: The Chapter on "Getting Started" will provide you with the step-by-step procedure to progress from the amateur level to college level and professional level of sports officiatings.

You may also refer to Appendix E, which is a listing of private officiating schools and accredited college-level officiating courses throughout the United States. Also, in Appendix B you will find a listing of college conferences and other football associations throughout the United States.

Appendix C will provide you with professional associations that utilize the majority of professional officials.

Publications and periodicals are located in Appendix D. They will provide the serious individual with additional background and critical information on the sport.

The major manufacturers of sports-related equipment and supplies can be found in Appendix F. Each sport will require its officials to possess a proper uniform and other officiating equipment. These manufacturers can save you a tremendous amount of time and effort in locating exactly the right pieces of equipment.

COMPENSATION: At the recreational level or intramural programs, salaries start at $10 per game. Salaries for junior high school officials start at $17.50 to $30 per official (with two or three officials being used), and for high school junior varsity level the range is $20 to $38 per official and varsity level (using seven officials) ranges from $35 to

$50 for the referee, and all other officials range between $18 to $50 per game. When a high school game of football is locally televised, officials' fee compensation is typically as follows: Play-by-play announcer $150, color commentator $100, statistician $50, field officials $30 each if a four-man crew, clock operator, field announcer, game statistician and security $22 each, chain gang and ball boy $9 each.

Salaries for college officials usually range from $200 to $300 per game depending upon experience, knowledge and rate standing, plus 50 cents per mile when the event is more than 200 miles away and per diem expenses. Statisticians, scorers and timers generally range from $20 to $30 per game.

For NCAA play offs, Divisions I-AA, II and III, each man will receive a minimum of $175 per game plus travel and per diem. For the Big Five Bowl officials (Rose Bowl, Cotton Bowl, Orange Bowl, Sugar Bowl and Fiesta Bowl), officials receive a fee of $400 per man, except those who work the Fiesta Bowl, which is slightly less.

At the Pro level (NFL), minor officials such as timekeepers, statisticians, chain crews, etc., can range from $35 to $100. Major officials receive anywhere from $450 to $1,300 per game. It should be understood that these officials have acquired a wealth of solid, practical experience plus the necessary rating and recommendations. USFL officials receive $400 per game as compensation.

NOTE: The NFL holds a series of playoff games. Officials who participate in such events are compensated $3,000 per game.

For the most watched professional football game, the Super Bowl, each of the seven-man crew receives a minimum fee of $5,000 plus travel and per diem expenses.

GENERAL QUESTIONS PERTAINING TO FOOTBALL

1. A touchdown is counted as six points. (T) or (F)
2. An extra point after a touchdown will count as one point. (T) or (F)
3. A field goal will count as three points. (T) or (F)
4. A forward pass that strikes an official standing inbounds, rebounds into the air and is caught by either team is considered a "live" ball. (T) or (F)
5. During the try for the extra point, the place kicker hits another player inside the neutral zone and the ball rebounds and passes through the upright poles but above the crossbar, the point is ruled good. (T) or (F)
6. During the kick-off, if the ball travels ten yards and is touched by the opposing team, the ball is considered to be "live." (T) or (F)
7. If a defensive player bumps or pushes the offensive receiver before the ball touches his hand, this is illegal. (T) or (F)
8. If the offensive line charges out before the ball is snapped, this is ruled illegal procedure. (T) or (F)
9. If the defensive line charges out before the ball is snapped, this is ruled off sides. (T) or (F)
10. If a forward pass touches a defensive player and is subsequently caught by another defensive player, the ball shall remain live. (T) or (F)
11. Each side shall consist of 11 players at the start of the game. (T) or (F)
12. An offensive team must travel at least 10 yards for a first down. (T) or (F)
13. An offensive team has a maximum of four downs to travel 10 yards. (T) or (F)
14. A line judge and umpire should retrieve any kicked ball. (T) or (F)
15. Spearing, butt blocking and face/head tackling are all illegal. (T) or (F)
16. A "safety" is awarded a maximum of two points. (T) or (F)
17. If an offensive back is tackled by any defensive player and the ball is dropped before the whistle blows, this is ruled a fumble or live ball. (T) or (F)
18. When an official blows his whistle, all play is to be stopped on the field. (T) or (F)
19. On major clock stoppers (such as: end of period, charge time-out, ball ruled out-of-bounds, incompleted pass, any score, touchback

or fair catch), the clock will not be restarted until the snap or free kick of the next play is performed. (T) or (F)

20. On minor clock stoppers (such as: a foul, official's time-out for first down or measuring of the first down, changing of possession, equipment repair, coach/official conference not chargeable to the coach, injured player), the clock will restart on the "ready for play" signal. (T) or (F)

Answers to Football Quiz

1. True
2. True
3. True
4. True
5. True
6. True
7. True
8. True
9. True
10. True
11. True
12. True
13. True
14. True
15. True
16. True
17. True
18. True
19. True
20. True

NATIONAL FEDERATION OF STATE HIGH SCHOOL ASSOCIATIONS FOOTBALL OFFICIAL SIGNALS

A football official must know and be able to demonstrate the officially accepted signals. Each of the following drawings represents one specific signal that is utilized during an official game. Attempt to identify (name) the signal depicted in each drawing. Compare your answers to the correct answers located at the end of the chapter.

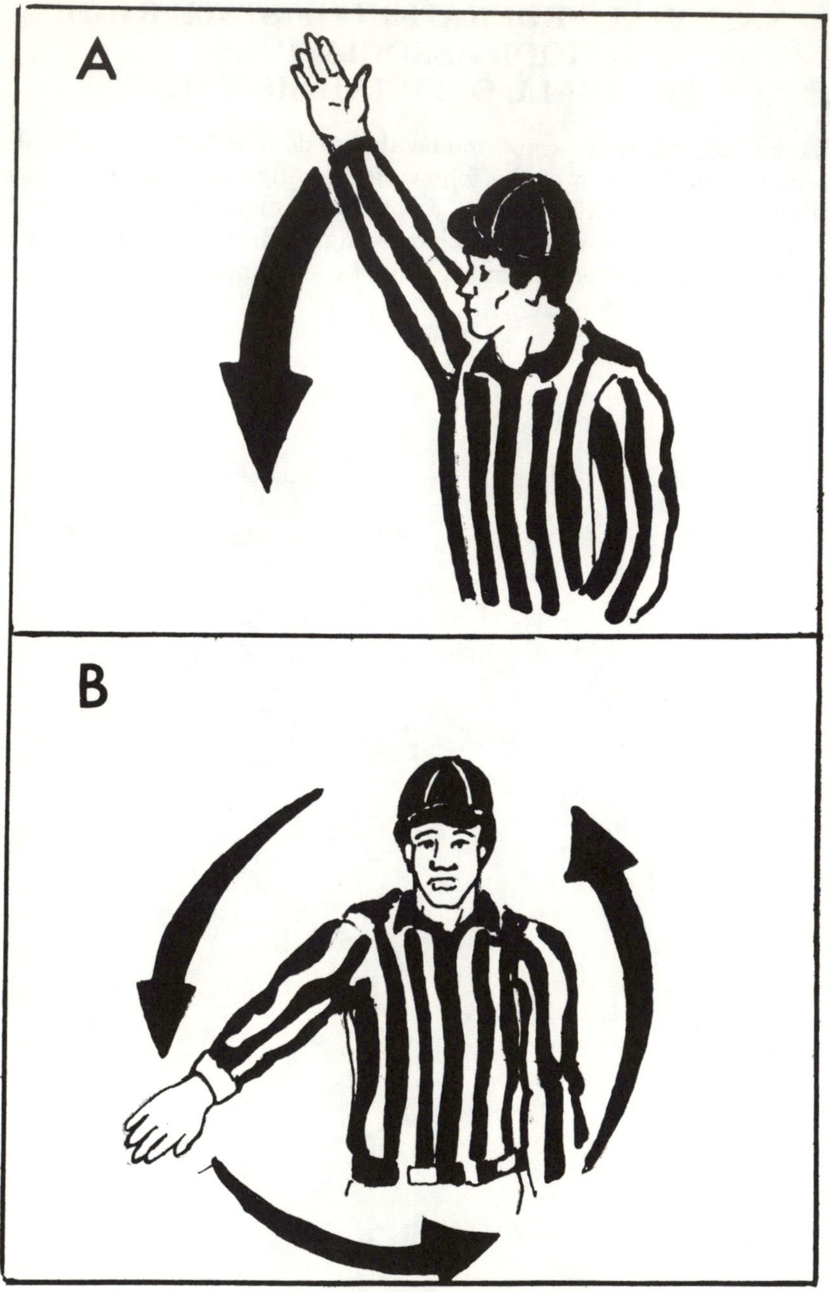
A
B

C

D

E

F

G

H

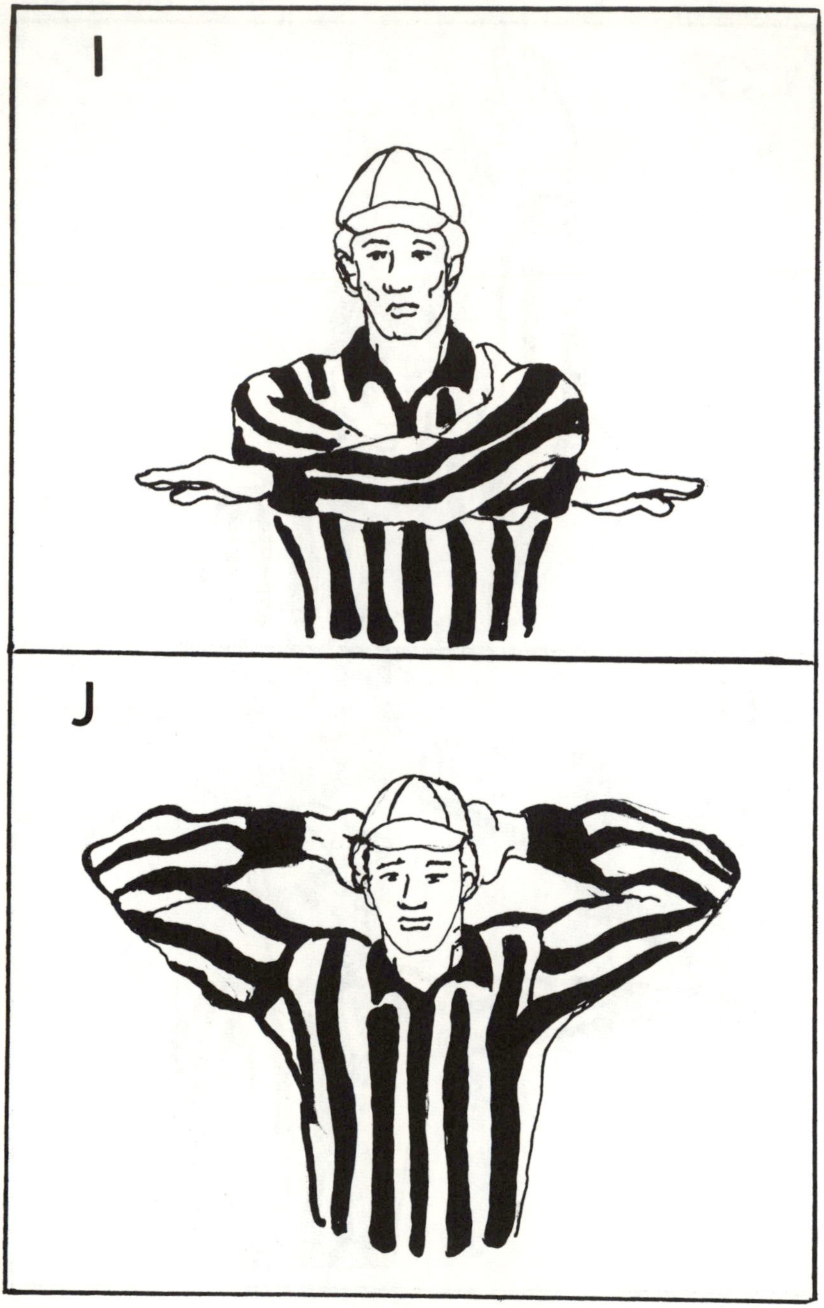
I
J

K

L

M
N

O

P

Q

R

S

T

U

V

W

X

Y
Z

AA

BB

CC

DD

EE

FF

GG

HH

II

JJ

KK

LL

MM

NN

OO

SIGNAL ANSWERS (Football):

A. Ball ready for play
B. Start clock
C. Time-out discretionary or injury time-out (follow by tapping hands on chest)
D. TV Time-out
E. Touchdown, Field Goal, Point(s) after Touchdown
F. Safety
G. Ball Dead, Touchback (move side to side)
H. First down
I. Incomplete forward pass, penalty decline, No play, No score
J. Loss of down
K. Legal touching of forward pass or scrimmage kick
L. Inadvertent whistle, (Face Press Box)
M. Disregard Flag
N. End of Period
O. Encroachment offside
P. Illegal procedure, False start, Illegal position
Q. Illegal motion, Illegal shift
R. Delay of game
S. Substitution infraction
T. Failure to wear required equipment
U. Grasping face mask or helmet opening
V. Player disqualification
W. Illegal use of hands or arms
X. Helping runner, interlocked interference
Y. Holding or obstructing
Z. Chop block
AA. Clipping
BB. Blocking below the waist, illegal block
CC. Ineligible downfield on pass
DD. Personal Foul
EE. Illegal pass, Illegal forward handling
FF. Intentional grounding
GG. Forward pass interference, Kick catching interference
HH. Roughing passer
II. Ball illegally kicked, batted or touched
JJ. Invalid fair catch signal, illegal fair catch signal
KK. Sideline interference
LL. Roughing kicker or holder

MM. Unsportsmanlike conduct, Noncontact Foul
NN. Illegal participation
OO. Tripping

CHAPTER X

ICE HOCKEY

Ice Hockey has earned a reputation for being fast moving and rough. Countless numbers of players and sometimes officials are injured each year. Therefore, there is a need for highly skilled, well disciplined officials who can command respect and maintain order before, during and after the game.

The game of hockey originated in Canada in the mid-1800s. It had become Canada's national sport by the early 1900s. Since that time, hockey has become a popular sport in the United States, Russia, Czechoslovakia and Sweden. Hockey is a recognized sport in the Winter Games of the Olympics.

In the United States and Canada, hockey is a popular amateur sport. It is played as a part of community, high school and college sports programs. The high schools and college teams in the United States play by a special set of rules which were formulated by the NCAA. All other amateur teams play by rules similar to professional hockey rules. Rules governing amateur ice hockey are set down by the Amateur Hockey Association of the United States (AHAUS). The game is played on an ice rink with a playing surface not less than 85 feet wide by 185 feet in length. The playing surface is required to be enclosed, and this enclosure (known as "boards") should not be less than 40 inches in height, but not more than 48 inches above the surface. There are over 600,000 registered amateur hockey players in Canada and 250,000 in the United States.

There is only one professional hockey major league, the National Hockey League (NHL), which was formed in Montreal, Canada in 1917. There are several minor leagues in the United States. The major league teams represent cities from both the United States and Canada. Each minor league team is usually affiliated with a major league team and serves as a training center for the new players.

The professional hockey season lasts from October to June, with a total of 40 officials and 630 players attempting to lead their respective team all the way to the Stanley Cup Championship Series.

On every level from the amateur to the professional, there are usually nine officials used for each hockey game. The three chief officials are stationed on the ice with the players. They are the referee and two linesmen. The other officials work off the ice and include a game timekeeper, a penalty timekeeper, the official scorer, two goal judges and the statistician. Some amateur games use two referees and no linesmen.

DUTIES: The referee is generally responsible for supervising and controlling the game, including other game officials. For any disputes that may arise during play, he has the authority to make the final decision, and impose prescribed penalties for rule infractions.

The lineman's main duty is to determine any infractions of the rules. These may include offside play or any violations pertaining to "trapping" or "icing the puck" regulations.

The linesman is primarily responsible for stopping play when the puck travels outside the rink. However, a linesman is not permitted to stop play to impose a penalty beyond his jurisdiction. It should be noted that in high school play, a linesman is not regularly utilized.

The goal judges (one for each goal) cannot be members of either team, and should remain isolated from spectators. Once assigned to a specific goal, they do not switch places with each other during the game. Primarily, it is the goal judge who must signal the referee when the puck has entered the goal cage, but the goal judge does not award a goal, this is strictly the referee's authority.

Because of the need to monitor the penalties, the penalty timekeeper is responsible for keeping a correct record of all penalties imposed by other officials, the nature of the penalties and names of those who have committed the infractions. In addition, the penalty timekeeper shall keep the time imposed on any penalized player as well as the posting of the penalty on the scoreboard. Any discrepancy between the time recorded on the clock and the official correct time shall be promptly brought to the attention of the referee.

The official scorer is responsible for obtaining a complete list of eligible players including the starting lineup from each team coach or manager before the game is started. The official scorer shall obtain the names of each captain (identified by a "C") and assigned alternates (identified by the letter "A"). The information is presented to the referee for his signature upon the completion of the game. In addition, the official scorer shall be responsible for maintaining a record of the goals scored, who scored the goal and those receiving credit for any assist. The official scorer shall prepare the official score sheet for the referee's signature so that it can be forwarded to the proper authorities. An up-to-date National Federation Ice Hockey Rule Book should be readily available at the scorer's table during the game.

Game time duration will vary between high school, amateur ice hockey, college and professional play. You should consult a specific rule book for specific time differences. For example: high school consists of three periods per game, each consisting of 15 minutes apiece of actual play, and no less than 10 minutes intermission between periods, and time outs shall be one minute; at the amateur level, each play period may be 20 minutes in duration, with a 15 minute intermission between periods.

The game timekeeper is responsible for signaling the referee for the start of the game as well as each succeeding period. He will also issue the preliminary warning signal (approximately three minutes) prior to the resumption of the game during the intermission. In addition, it is his responsibility to announce the appropriate time in each period, including a one minute remaining signal in regulation play. This may be accomplished by an automatic gong, bell, siren, or in some cases if this equipment is not available, by blowing a whistle. Should a dispute occur pertaining to time, the referee will determine the final decision.

SPECIAL QUALIFICATIONS: Officials must be able to skate with an advanced level of proficiency. The AHAUS and professional hockey associations seek individuals who are mature, intelligent, level-headed and even tempered as well as those who have the ability to deal with others in a reasonable manner. To qualify for membership in AHAUS, an applicant must pass an open book test as well as a skating test. Clinics and seminars are also required to be attended on a regular basis. Recommendations and references attesting to previous experience will be requested at the time of registering for membership.

How to become an Ice Hockey official: The **first step** in the process is to contact your State High School Athletic Association or the National Federation of State High School Athletic Associations and request an application and official rule book of regulations pertaining to Ice Hockey. At the same time, the **second step** is to request information pertaining to a listing of accredited local agencies or approved class training stations in your geographical area. You should make plans to attend the next open session when it becomes available. The **third step** is to study the materials so that you will be able to pass the written and practical examination. The **fourth step** is to apply for membership in one or more of the appropriate associations. The necessary information can be obtained by asking your State High School Athletic Association, the Federation of State High School Athletic Associations or local agencies for their recommendations. See Appendix A which is a listing of all the state high school associations throughout the United States.

Applications take approximately two weeks to process. Fees will normally range between $10 and $20.

During this interim, contact your area recreational director(s), your junior high and high school ice hockey coach, and volunteer to observe and/or officiate with these types of community programs, or at the intramural level. Your involvement will provide you with invaluable practical experience.

NOTE: The Chapter on "Getting Started" will provide you with the step-by-step procedure to progress from the amateur level to college level and professional level of sports officiating.

You may also refer to Appendix E, which is a listing of private officiating schools and accredited college-level officiating courses throughout the United States. Also, in Appendix B you will find a listing of college conferences and other ice hockey associations throughout the United States.

Appendix C will provide you with professional associations that utilize the majority of professional officials.

Publications and periodicals are located in Appendix D. They will provide the serious individual with additional background and critical information on the sport.

The major manufacturers of sports-related equipment and supplies can be found in Appendix F. Each sport will require its officials to possess a proper uniform and other officiating equipment. These manufacturers can save you a tremendous amount of time and effort in locating exactly the right piece of equipment.

COMPENSATION: At the recreational level or intramural programs, salaries start at $15 per game. Salaries for junior high school officials start at $20 per official, and for high school junior varsity level is $25 per official and varsity level $30 per official.

Salaries at the collegiate level for each Referee range from $150 to $180 per game and higher depending upon experience, knowledge and rate standing.

NOTE: NCAA men's championship Divisions I, II and III officials (two referees) are usually paid $300 to $360 per game, and one linesman,

$60 per game, two Goal Judges, $25 per game, and one Alternate, $20, plus per diem and travel expenses. Official Scorers and Game Timekeeper will generally range from $20 to $70 based upon experience.

At the professional level, officials must be registered and qualified. Once an official has achieved this status and is qualified to be an NHL official, the compensation package is generous and liberal. Salaries for referees range from $36,000 to $75,000 and linesmen are paid from $24,000 to $50,000, plus per diem and travel expenses.

GENERAL QUESTIONS PERTAINING TO ICE HOCKEY

1. A goal is made when the puck, entering from the front, passes between the goal posts, below the top of the net and completely crosses the goal line. (T) or (F)
2. A goal should not be allowed if (a) the puck is kicked, (b) thrown, (c) carried, or (d) strikes an official prior to entering the net. (T) or (F)
3. All goals scored shall count as one point. (T) or (F)
4. An "assist" shall be credited to the player or players taking part in the play immediately preceding the scoring of a goal. (T) or (F)
5. A "save" for a goalkeeper shall be credited only when the goalkeeper has prevented the puck from entering the net. (T) or (F)
6. Only team captains have the privilege of speaking or communicating with the Referee. (T) or (F)
7. No player shall intentionally touch, trip, hold or push an official during, before or after a game. (T) or (F)
8. It is illegal for coaches or managers to use whistles or other mechanical equipment to signal instructions to their team of players. (T) or (F)
9. Any player will be disqualified if the following occur: (a) fighting, (b) spearing, (c) kicking or (d) grabbing face protectors. (T) or (F)
10. If a player commits a "major" infraction, the penalty time shall be 4 minutes of actual playing time. (T) or (F)

Listed below are affiliate organizations throughout the country that are members of the Amateur Hockey Association of the United States (AHAUS). Collectively, these organizations have more than 11,300 hockey teams that are registered with AHAUS. If you can meet the initial requirements (especially the ability to ice skate), it would be in your interest to become an active member of AHAUS.

ALASKA STATE HOCKEY ASSOCIATION, P. O. Box 6721, Anchorage, AK 99502

ATLANTIC AMATEUR HOCKEY ASSOCIATION, 3130 Walnut Ave., Philadelphia, PA 19130

CALIFORNIA AMATEUR HOCKEY ASSOCIATION, 23942 Sunset Crossing, Diamond Bar, CA 91765

CONNECTICUT HOCKEY CONFERENCE, 47 Breezy Hill, South Windsor, CT 06074

AMATEUR HOCKEY ASSOCIATION ILLINOIS, INC., 1108 Plum Grove Road, Schaumburg, IL 60195

MAINE AMATEUR HOCKEY ASSOCIATION, 54 Pine Street, Box 587, Lewiston, ME 04140

AMATEUR HOCKEY ASSOCIATION COMMON-WEALTH OF MASSACHUSETTS, 26 Burley Street, Wenham, MA 01984

MICHIGAN AMATEUR HOCKEY ASSOCIATION, P. O. Box 504, St. Clair Shores, MI 48083

MID-AMERICAN HOCKEY ASSOCIATION, 408 Becker Drive, Pittsburgh, PA 15237

MINNESOTA AMATEUR HOCKEY ASSOCIATION, 501 3rd Avenue SE, Minneapolis, MN 55414

MISSOURI AMATEUR HOCKEY ASSOCIATION, 413 Webster Forest, Webster Groves, MO 63119

NEW HAMPSHIRE AMATEUR HOCKEY ASSOCIATION, Mack Hill Road, Amherst, NH 03031

NEW YORK STATE AMATEUR HOCKEY ASSOCIATION, INC., P. O. Box 307, Lewiston, NY 14902

NORTH DAKOTA AMATEUR HOCKEY ASSOCIATION, 1517 Griggs, Grafton, ND 58237

PACIFIC NORTHWEST AMATEUR ASSOCIATION, 5225 West Clearwater, B-6, Kennewick, WA 99336

RHODE ISLAND AMATEUR HOCKEY ASSOCIATION, 84 Allerton Avenue, East Providence, RI 02914

ROCKEY MOUNTAIN/SOUTHWEST AMATEUR HOCKEY ASSOCIATION, (Arizona Registrar) 1620 Entrada Once, Tuscon, AZ 86001; (Colorado Registrar) 8641 Circle Drive, Westminster, CO 80030; (Idaho Registrar) 580 Safstrom, Idaho Falls, ID 83401; (Montana Registrar) 100 North 27th Street, #400, Billings, MT 59101; (New Mexico Registrar) 1413 Hoffman Avenue, Albuquerque, NM 87110; (Oklahoma Registrar) 4372 E. 57th Street, Tulsa, OK 74135; (Texas Registrar) 605 Winchester Dr., Richardson, TX 75080; (Utah Registrar) 2001 South 700 East, Salt Lake City, UT 84105

SOUTHEAST AMATEUR HOCKEY ASSOCIATION, P. O. Box 5208, Takoma Park, MD 20912

SOUTH DAKOTA AMATEUR HOCKEY ASSOCIATION, Mina, SD 57462

VERMONT AMATEUR HOCKEY ASSOCIATION, 35 Beverly Court, St. Albans, VT 05478

WISCONSIN AMATEUR HOCKEY ASSOCIATION, White Pine Drive, Eagle River, WI 54521

Answers To Ice Hockey Quiz

1. True
2. True
3. True
4. True
5. True
6. True
7. True
8. True
9. True
10. True

NATIONAL FEDERATION OF STATE HIGH SCHOOL ASSOCIATIONS ICE HOCKEY OFFICIAL SIGNALS

An ice hockey official must know and be able to demonstrate the officially accepted signals. Each of the following drawings represents one specific signal that is utilized during an official game. Attempt to identify (name) the signal depicted in each drawing. Compare your answers to the correct answers located at the end of the chapter.

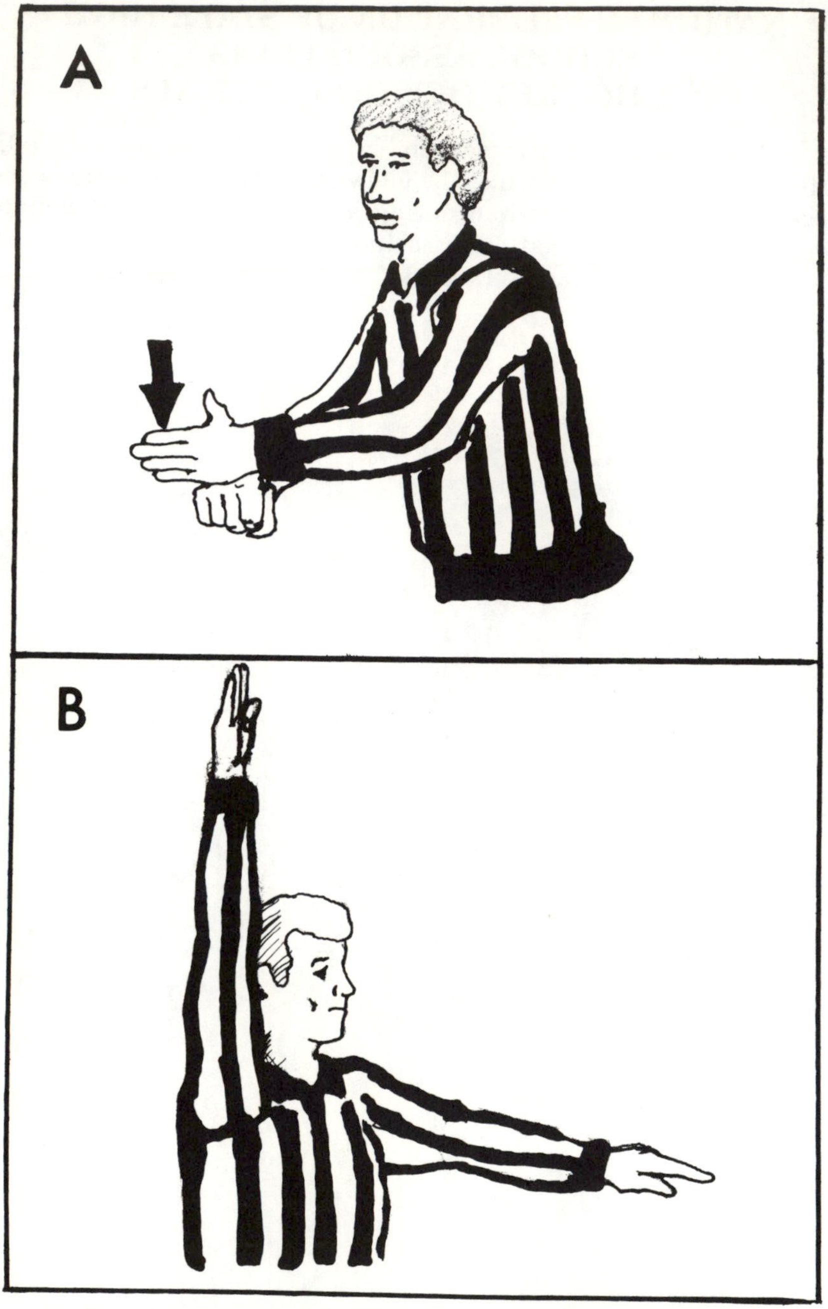
A
B

C

D

E

F

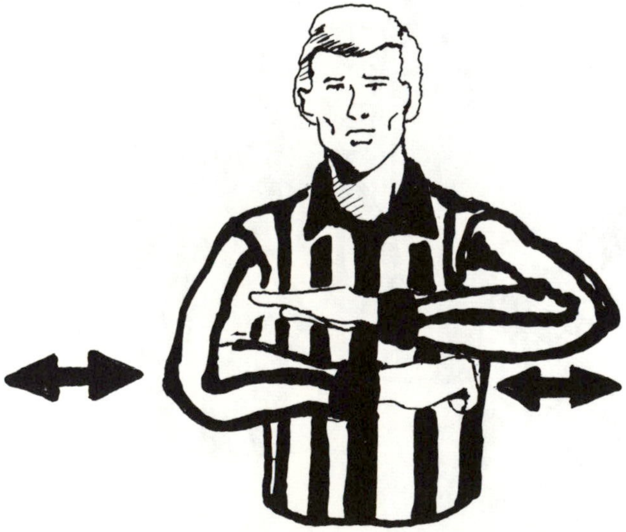

G

H

I

J

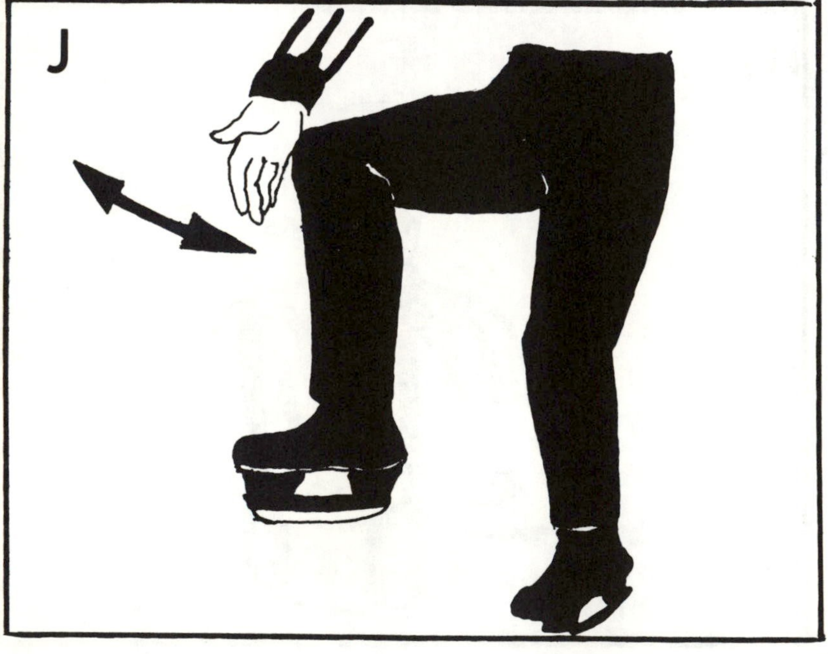

K

L

M
N

O

P

Q

R

S

T

U

V

W

X

Y

SIGNAL ANSWERS (Ice Hockey):

A. Slashing.
B. Delayed Calling of penalty.
C. Interference.
D. Hooking.
E. High-sticking.
F. Butt-ending.
G. Holding.
H. Icing.
I. Time-out.
J. Tripping.
K. Wash-out.
L. Checking from behind.
M. Delayed calling of penalty.
N. Penalty shot.
O. Misconduct.
P. Roughing & fighting.
Q. Kneeing.
R. Slow whistle.
S. Spearing.
T. Grasping face mask.
U. Charging.
V. Cross-checking and illegal use of hands.
W. Elbowing.
X. Boarding.
Y. Unsportsmanlike conduct.

CHAPTER XI

BOXING

Boxing is a brutal sport — in one form or another it has been around for approximately 2000 years. Boxers fight on both amateur and professional levels. The sport has enjoyed several periods of popularity, and its golden age in the United States was from the 1920s to the 1940s.

Muhammad Ali helped to arouse spectator interest to a new height during the 1960s and 70s. This renewed interest lead to the development of a multi-million dollar business where fighters were being promised earnings of millions of dollars for fighting one match. Boxing matches were being televised into millions of homes and also shown on closed-circuit or cable.

Most competitive amateur boxing in the United States is regulated by the Amateur Athletic Union (AAU). On the amateur level, boxing is a part of the sports program in many schools, boys' clubs and various branches of the Armed Forces. The AAU holds national championships every year and is responsible for supervising the U. S. Olympic boxing team.

The most famous amateur boxing competition is the Golden Gloves tournament. It is a national tournament with a series of state and regional eliminations that lead to the final bouts.

Professional boxers fight in matches arranged by a promoter. The promoter is responsible for making all necessary arrangements such as renting the arena, selling tickets, arranging for television and radio rights, and paying the boxers.

Professional boxing is regulated by state and local boxing commissions. Most of these commissions belong to the World Boxing Association, some to the World Boxing Council and others to both. The WBA and the WBC are international organizations but professional boxing in Canada is regulated by the Canadian Boxing Federation.

Each boxing match (amateur or professional) is officiated by one referee. It is his responsibility to see that the fighters obey the rules.

He has the authority to warn a boxer for a rule violation and later disqualify a boxer for too many violations or serious infractions. The referee can also stop a match if he determines that one of the boxers is unable to effectively compete physically.

Outside the ring, two or three judges score the match. Amateur championship fights require five judges. The timekeeper times the rounds and sounds the bell beginning and ending each round. The official ring physician is present to provide medical treatment if needed. When the referee is in doubt about stopping a fight, the physician advises him on the fighter's physical condition.

How to become a boxing official: The first step is to join the Official United States of America Amateur Boxing Federation (USA/ABF), 3400 West 86th Street, Indianapolis, IN 46268, and ask for their official rule book, an application and procedures. By contacting USA/ABF headquarters, you can obtain specific information pertaining to area affiliates or area Boxing Commissions that will assist you in qualifying for certification as an amateur boxing official. To successfully complete the certification procedure will require you to attend a series of boxing clinics and training camps.

After you have applied to the USA/ABF, contact your area recreational director(s) or the physical education instructor(s) with area gym facilities that have boxing programs, and volunteer to work with these types of programs. Your involvement will provide you with invaluable practical experience.

After you have obtained at least two years of practical experience, it is recommended that you also consider joining the Amateur International Boxing Association (AIBA). The application procedure for membership is available through USA/ABF listed above. The AIBA organization consists of world-class officials, and opportunities are greater for qualified members for international and national tournaments.

At the professional level, appointments are made by the district president of the USA/ABF and AIBA. Letters of recommendation are mandatory from these officials before you can perform as a professional boxing official. All interested candidates should write to their State Boxing Commission for the individual state's application forms, including laws and rules that regulate boxing matches.

Once you have become a member of the State Boxing Commission, the next step is to join the four major professional boxing associations. Your membership in these organizations will make you eligible for official employment. Telephone numbers and addresses can be obtained from your state's Boxing Commission for the following professional organizations:

THE WORLD BOXING COUNCIL (WBC),

THE WORLD BOXING ASSOCIATION (WBA)

NORTH AMERICAN BOXING FEDERATION (NABF)

INTERNATIONAL BOXING FEDERATION (IBF)

Regular boxing bouts consist of two referees, three judges, one official timer and one inspector. The number of officials being used per bout will vary depending upon the number of matches and the size of the boxing event.

COMPENSATION: Amateur referees' salaries range from $20 to $35. Amateur judging officials range from $15 to $20. Timekeepers are compensated from $15 to $20, and inspectors usually receive $20. All the salaries will be governed by the amount of amateur officiating experience.

Professional compensation for World Title Fights: Referee — approximately $1,200 plus travel and expenses for each match. Judge — $850 for each of the three officials. All other officials usually receive $75 to $100 per match. If the match is televised, Timers and Inspectors will receive $800 each.

NOTE: Officials are selected by one of the top four associations (WBC, WBA, NABF and IBF).

Local, regional and divisional professional matches are compensated less than the above pay scales, especially when the event is not televised. For example: Referees — $100 to $150, Judges — $75 to $100, and other officials approximately the same. Officials who regularly cover World Class professional fights average between $15,000 and 20,000 annually plus travel expenses.

QUESTIONS PERTAINING TO BOXING

1. A knock-out or KO occurs when a fighter is knocked down and does not stand up within 10 seconds. (T) or (F)
2. Outfighting is boxing at long range. (T) or (F)
3. A foul is an unsportsmanlike action that can seriously injure an opponent. (T) or (F)
4. Infighting is boxing at close range. (T) or (F)
5. Neutral Corners are the corners of the ring not occupied by either boxer and their respective trainers between rounds. (T) or (F)
6. Technical knockout or TKO is scored when the referee decides that a fighter cannot continue the fight, although he has not been officially knocked out. (T) or (F)
7. It is legal for a fighter to use his feet. (T) or (F)
8. Hitting below the belt line is a good boxing tactic. (T) or (F)
9. Holding an opponent's arm while punching him is legal in professional matches only. (T) or (F)
10. Using the elbows is considered a legal tactic. (T) or (F)

Answers To Boxing Quiz

1. True
2. True
3. True
4. True
5. True
6. True
7. False
8. False
9. False
10. False

CHAPTER XII

WRESTLING

The fast action and confined area of competitive wrestling (not to be confused with the theatrical wrestling) requires a referee official who moves quickly and accurately around the participants.

Rules and regulations governing the sport are available in a current copy of the Official Wrestling Guide which is available through either the State High School Athletic Association or the National Collegiate Athletic Association. An up to date official guide will contain numerous suggestions as well as current requirements for working in competitive wrestling.

In addition to being a qualified official which can only come from practical experience, a referee official should conduct a series of pre-match inspections involving the facility and equipment being used on the junior high, high school and college levels, officials should consult with each team's coach to review the rules or rule changes that may affect the match.

In championship meets, referee officials will also conduct weight-in inspections using beam-weight platform scales or swinging-arm spring-balance scales. Naturally, the scale itself should be inspected before the true weights of the participants can be attested. In addition to a referee, major competition events utilize the services of a mat judge, assistant referee, scorekeeper and timekeeper. These situations will require the officials to hold a pre-match meeting to clarify signals to be used.

At the start of the match, it is the referee's duty to instruct each contestant at the center of the mat. Such instructions will generally consist of when to break, what to do at the command of the whistle, and where to hold the action to remain as near the center of the mat as possible.

A match is initiated by a hand-whistle signal while both participants are standing on their feet. In the two subsequent rounds, players will alternate their starting positions on the mat.

Due to the nature of this physical contact sport, players should be cautioned by the referee against using potentially dangerous tactics or holds. Those seen on television rarely comply with true competitive wrestling standards, and participants should be warned against the use of non-standard tactics in order to prevent serious bodily injury.

How to become a Wrestling official: The **first step** in the process is to contact your State High School Athletic Association or the National Federation of State High School Athletic Associations and request an application and official rule book of regulations pertaining to Wrestling. At the same time, the **second step** is to request information pertaining to a listing of accredited local agencies or approved class training stations in your geographical area. You should make plans to attend the next open session. The **third step** is to study the materials so that you will be able to pass the written and practical examination. The **fourth step** is to apply for membership in one or more of the appropriate associations. The necessary information can be obtained by asking your State High School Athletic Association, the Federation of State High School Athletic Associations or local agencies for their recommendations. See Appendix A, which is a listing of all the state high school associations throughout the United States.

Applications take approximately two weeks to process. Fees will normally range between $10 and $20.

During this interim, contact your area recreational director(s), your junior high and high school wrestling coach, and volunteer to observe and/or officiate with these types of community programs, or at the intramural level. Your involvement will provide you with invaluable practical experience.

NOTE: The Chapter on "Getting Started" will provide you with the step-by-step procedure to progress from the amateur level to college level and to the professional level of sports officiating.

You may also refer to Appendix E, which is a listing of private officiating schools and accredited college-level officiating courses throughout the United States. Also, in Appendix B you will find a listing of college conferences and other associations throughout the United States pertaining to Wrestling.

Publications and periodicals are located in Appendix D. They will provide the serious individual with additional background and critical information.

The major manufacturers of sports-related equipment and supplies can be found in Appendix F. Each sport will require its officials to possess a proper uniform and other officiating equipment. These manufacturers can save you a tremendous amount of time and effort in locating exactly the right piece of equipment.

COMPENSATION: At the junior high and recreational levels, compensation ranges from $10 to $20 per official; at the high school level, junior varsity officials range from $18 to $20; varsity competition ranges from $30 to $35. At the college level, compensation starts at $50 to $100 per official based upon experience.

Compensation for scorers and timers at the amateur level starts at $10 to $25, and at the college level, $25 and above depending upon experience.

Professional Wrestling is only exhibition, but compensation for referees ranges from $60 to $150. For additional information pertaining to professional wrestling, contact your state wrestling commission.

GENERAL QUESTIONS PERTAINING TO WRESTLING

1. There is no limit to the amount of time outs that may be called when a wrestler has been injured. (T) or (F)
2. The maximum amount of time allowed for an injured contestant is three minutes. (T) or (F)
3. If a wrestler has been accidentally injured and cannot complete the match, the match is canceled and the official will declare a draw. (T) or (F)
4. When a takedown has been earned, the official will award two match points. (T) or (F)
5. When the defensive wrestler earns an escape, the official will award two points. (T) or (F)
6. The defensive wrestler who successfully gains a reversal is awarded two points. (T) or (F)
7. For the following situations in a dual meet, "Fall, Forfeit, Default and Disqualification," the official (referee) will award six points. (T) or (F)
8. When indicating an infraction, the referee shall stop the match with the following exceptions: (a) warning the offensive or defensive wrestler for stalling, (b) penalizing the defensive wrestler for stalling, (c) in a pinning situation to penalize the defensive wrestler and (d) locked hands or grasping of clothing by the offensive wrestler while the defensive wrestler is attempting an escape or reversal. (T) or (F)
9. It is permissible for either wrestler to wear moustaches or beards. (T) or (F)
10. With respect to a referee's clothing, other than wearing a short-sleeve shirt, there is no official dress code required. (T) or (F)

Answers To Wrestling Quiz

1. True
2. False
3. False
4. True
5. False
6. True
7. True
8. True
9. False
10. False

NATIONAL FEDERATION OF STATE HIGH SCHOOL ASSOCIATIONS WRESTLING OFFICIAL SIGNALS

A wrestling official must know and be able to demonstrate the officially accepted signals. Each of the following drawings represents one specific signal that is utilized during an official game. Attempt to identify (name) the signal depicted in each drawing. Compare your answers to the correct answers located at the end of the chapter.

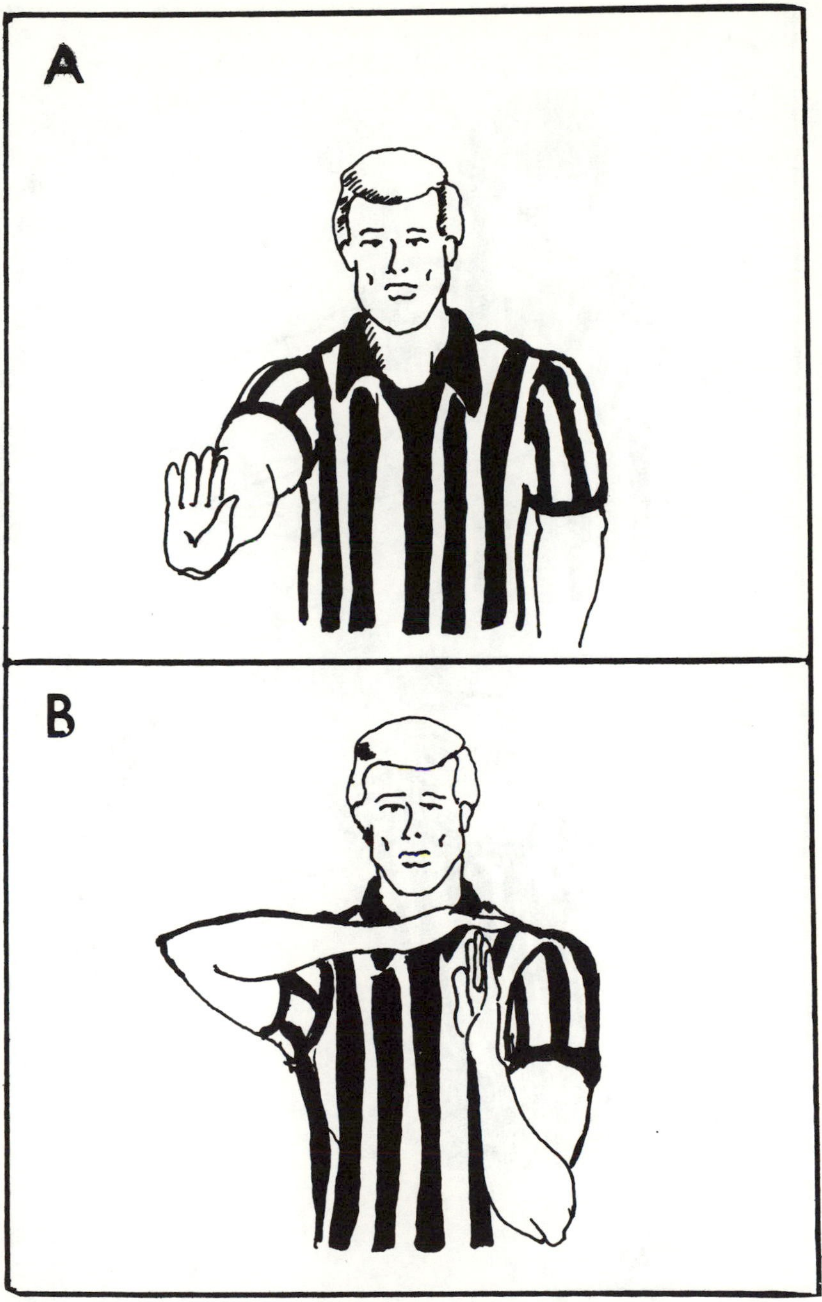
A
B

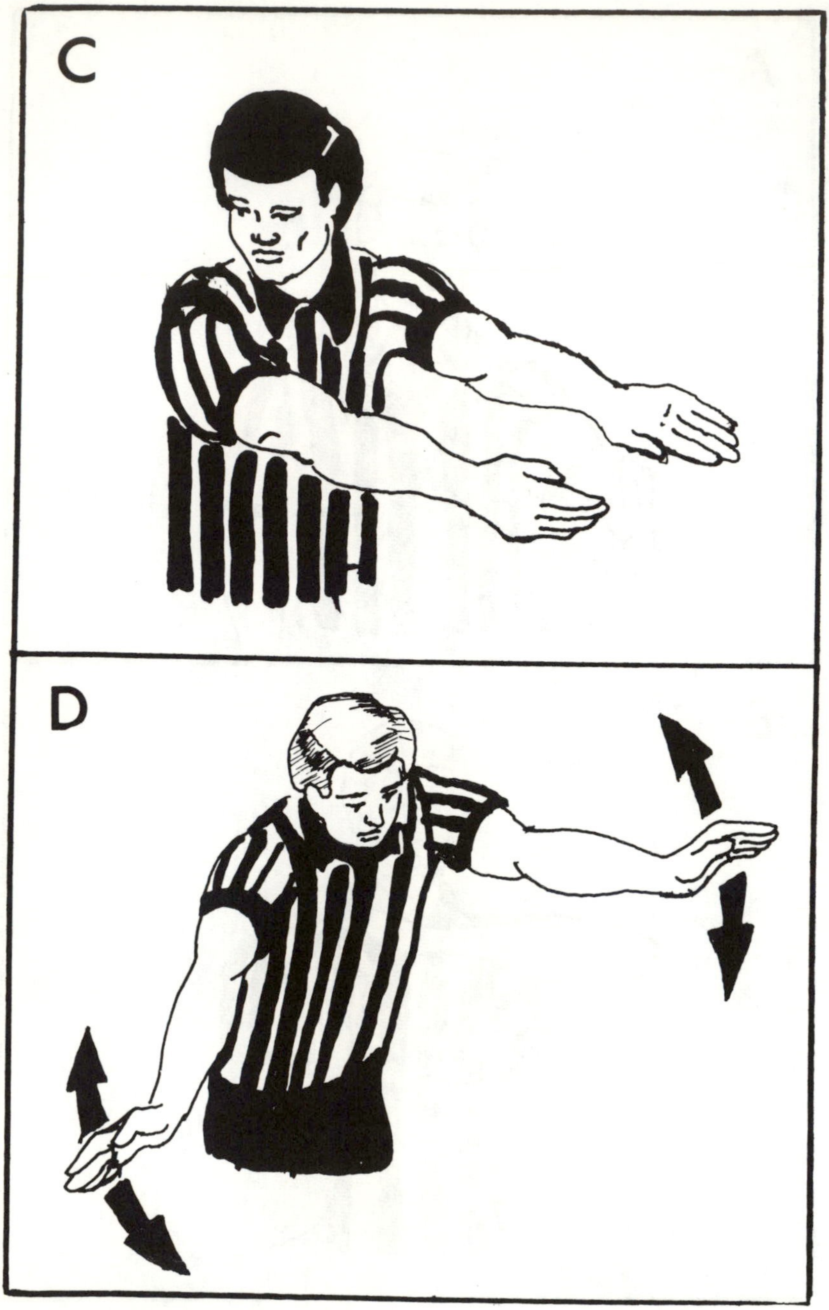
C
D

E

F

G

H

I

J

K

L

M

N

O

P

a

SIGNAL ANSWERS (Wrestling):

A. Stopping the Match
B. Technical Violation and Misconduct
C. Out-of-Bounds
D. Indicating No Control
E. Awarding Points
F. Reversal
G. Interlocking Hands or Grasping Clothing
H. Near — Fall
I. Caution for False Start
J. Warning
K. Illegal Hold
L. Indicating Wrestler in Control
M. Stalemate
N. Time Out
O. Neutral Position
P. Potentially Dangerous Hold
Q. Unsportsmanlike conduct and Flagrant Misconduct

CHAPTER XIII

SOCCER

By many, soccer is considered the world's most popular sport. Millions of people in more than 140 countries play the game. It is the national sport of most Latin American and European countries. The World Cup Championship is the most well-known international tournament and is held every four years.

In countries other than the United States, soccer is often referred to as football. The game was developed in England during the 1800s. It did not become popular in the United States until the mid-1900s. Now, it is considered one of the country's fastest growing sports. In the United States it is played by all ages. There are community leagues, high school, college and professional leagues.

The Federation Internationale de Football Association (FIFA) governs the play of soccer throughout the world and most soccer games are played by their rules, including games in the United States and Canada. The United States Soccer Federation (USSF), the Canadian Soccer Association (CSA) and 138 other countries are members of the FIFA.

As of 1984, the United States had two major professional soccer leagues: the North American Soccer League (NASL) and the Major Indoor Soccer League (MISL). The NASL consists of 20 teams that represent cities in both the United States and Canada. The MISL has 14 teams and they play their season entirely indoors.

The United States Youth Soccer Association (USYSA) is a division of the USSF and sponsors state, regional and national championships for youth.

A few countries in Europe and Latin America have professional and semi-professional leagues. These leagues are divided into divisions based on the team's playing ability. The winner of the top division is considered the national champion.

Twenty-four countries compete in the World Cup Championship, and all FIFA members can compete in the qualifying rounds held two years before the competition.

On the high school and college level, two referees or one referee and two linesmen are used for every soccer game. On the international and professional level, one referee and two linesmen are used. The referee's duties include keeping the time during the game and enforcing the rules. The referee has the authority to settle all disputes arising during the game and has the authority to eject a player from the game for repeated fouling. The linesmen decide possession of the ball and notify the referee of players committing fouls.

Similar to football, soccer is played by two opposing teams each consisting of 11 men. The ball is slightly larger in size than a regulation size volleyball, yet smaller than a regulation basketball. The game is primarily a kicking activity with only the goalkeepers permitted to intentionally handle the ball.

In regulation play, the game of soccer consists of two halves of 45 minutes in duration. Thus, total game time usually consists of 90 minutes. The time can be changed so long as each half is the same amount of time in duration except in situations requiring overtime.

Soccer is as physical as basketball or football, and it requires officials who can physically perform to keep on top of the action.

It is recommended that you apply to the State Referee Administrator or State Youth Referee Administrator. They can assign or recommend a recognized training program that will prepare a candidate for testing.

At the state and provincial (Canadian) levels, officials must be registered and qualified as either a State I or National Referee. This requirement is in addition to a personal recommendation from the State or Provincial Referee Administrators. Once an official has achieved this status and is qualified to be an MISL official, the compensation package is generous. A part-time official commands $150 per game, and a full-time official with experience can command $25,000-$40,000 plus per diem and travel expenses a year. Depending upon experience, some will be compensated slightly higher.

How to become a soccer official: The **first step** in the process is to contact your State High School Athletic Association or the National Federation of State High School Athletic Associations and request an application and official rule book of regulations pertaining to soccer. At the same time, the **second step** is to request information pertaining to a listing of accredited local agencies or approved class training stations in your geographical area. You should make plans to attend the next open session. The **third step** is to study the materials so that you will be able to pass the written and practical examination. The

fourth step is to apply for membership in one or more of the appropriate associations. The necessary information can be obtained by asking your State High School Athletic Association, the Federation of State High School Athletic Associations or local agencies for their recommendations. See Appendix A, which is a listing of all the state high school associations throughout the United States.

Applications take approximately two weeks to process. Fees will normally range between $10 and $20.

During this interim, contact your area recreational director(s), your junior high and high school soccer coach, and volunteer to observe and/or officiate with these types of community programs, or at the intramural level. Your involvement will provide you with invaluable practical experience.

NOTE: The chapter on "Getting Started" will provide you with the step-by-step procedure to progress from the amateur level to college level and professional level of sports officiatings.

You may also refer to Appendix E, which is a listing of private officiating schools and accredited college-level officiating courses throughout the United States. Also, in Appendix B you will find a listing of college conferences and other soccer associations throughout the United States. You should seriously consider joining one or more of these organizations to acquire official recognition.

Appendix C will provide you with professional associations that utilize the majority of professional officials.

Publications and periodicals are located in Appendix D. They will provide the serious individual with additional background and critical information on the sport.

The major manufacturers of sports-related equipment and supplies can be found in Appendix F. Each sport will require its officials to possess a proper uniform and other officiating equipment. These manufacturers can save you a tremendous amount of time and effort in locating exactly the right pieces of equipment.

COMPENSATION: At the recreational level or intramural programs, salaries start at $10 per game. Salaries for junior high school officials start at $17.50 per official, and high school junior varsity level is $20 per official and varsity level $22.50 per official.

Salaries for college officials will range from $45 to $60 per game and higher depending upon experience, knowledge and rate standing. NOTE: NCAA men's championship Divisions I, II and III officials (one referee and two linesmen) are usually paid $60 for referee and $40 for each linesman, plus per diem and travel expenses. Scorers and timers generally range from $20 to $30 based upon experience.

GENERAL QUESTIONS PERTAINING TO SOCCER

1. A goal is counted as two points. (T) or (F)
2. A goal may be scored during normal play directly from (a) a direct free kick, (b) penalty kick, (c) a corner kick, (d) dropped ball, and/or (e) goal-keeper's throw, punt or drop kick. (T) or (F)
3. A goal may be scored during normal play directly from (a) kicker of a kickoff, (b) indirect free kick, (c) goal kick, (d) throw-in, and/or (e) free kick into a team's own goal. (T) or (F)
4. A game shall be terminated if a team (a) refuses to play, and (b) has fewer than 11 players at the start of the game, or 7 players during the game. (T) or (F)
5. If the crossbar becomes displaced for any reason during the game, the ball shall be declared dead and official time is called. (T) or (F)
6. If the crossbar cannot be repaired or replaced in a reasonable length of time, the game shall continue. (T) or (F)
7. The score of a forfeited game shall be 1-0 if the game has not been started. (T) or (F)
8. A player should not be penalized for off-side position if the player receives the ball directly from (a) goal kick, (b) corner kick, (c) throw-in, and/or drop by an official. (T) or (F)
9. A player having one or both feet on the ground shall not charge into an opponent who has both feet off the ground. (T) or (F)
10. A player shall not hold, push or impede an opponent with the hand(s) or arm(s) extended from the body. (T) or (F)
11. A player should not place a hand(s) on an opponent in an effort to reach the ball. (T) or (F)
12. If a player is caught holding or pushing the penalty is an indirect "free" kick. (T) or (F)
13. A player should not charge into an opponent when neither player is within playing distance of the ball. (T) or (F)
14. An indirect free kick is awarded to an opponent if a player charges into the opponent within playing distance of the ball. (T) or (F)
15. A player or coach shall be cautioned for (a) coaching outside the team area, or (b) using coaching aids in excess. (T) or (F)
16. Indirect free kicks are declared if a player (a) trips or attempts to trip an opponent, (b) kicks or attempts to kick an opponent, and/or (c) charges an opponent in a violent or dangerous manner. (T) or (F)
17. Only the captain of an offended team may take (or make) the free kick. (T) or (F)

18. A penalty kick shall be awarded when a foul, which ordinarily results in the awarding of a direct free kick, occurs within the offending team's penalty area. (T) or (F)
19. Projecting metal or other types of hard plates, or projection on clothing or person are considered illegal equipment. (T) or (F)
20. When a player is removed for illegal equipment or uniform, there shall be no replacement until the next opportunity to make a substitution. (T) or (F)

Answers to Soccer Quiz

1. False
2. True
3. False
4. True
5. True
6. False
7. True
8. True
9. True
10. True
11. True
12. False
13. True
14. True
15. True
16. False
17. False
18. True
19. True
20. True

NATIONAL FEDERATION OF STATE HIGH SCHOOL ASSOCIATIONS SOCCER OFFICIAL SIGNALS

A soccer official must know and be able to demonstrate the officially accepted signals. Each of the following drawings represents one specific signal that is utilized during an official game. Attempt to identify (name) the signal depicted in each drawing. Compare your answers to the correct answers located at the end of the chapter.

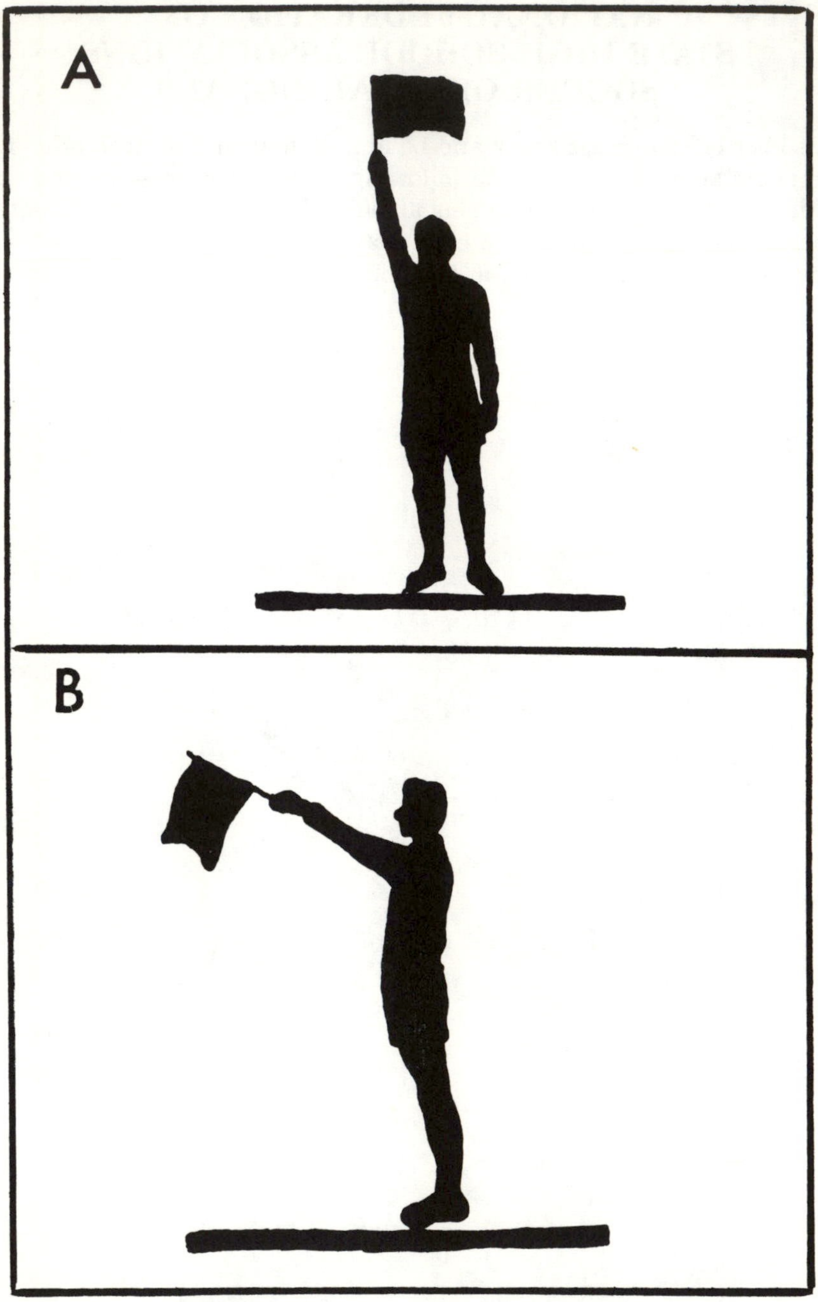
A
B

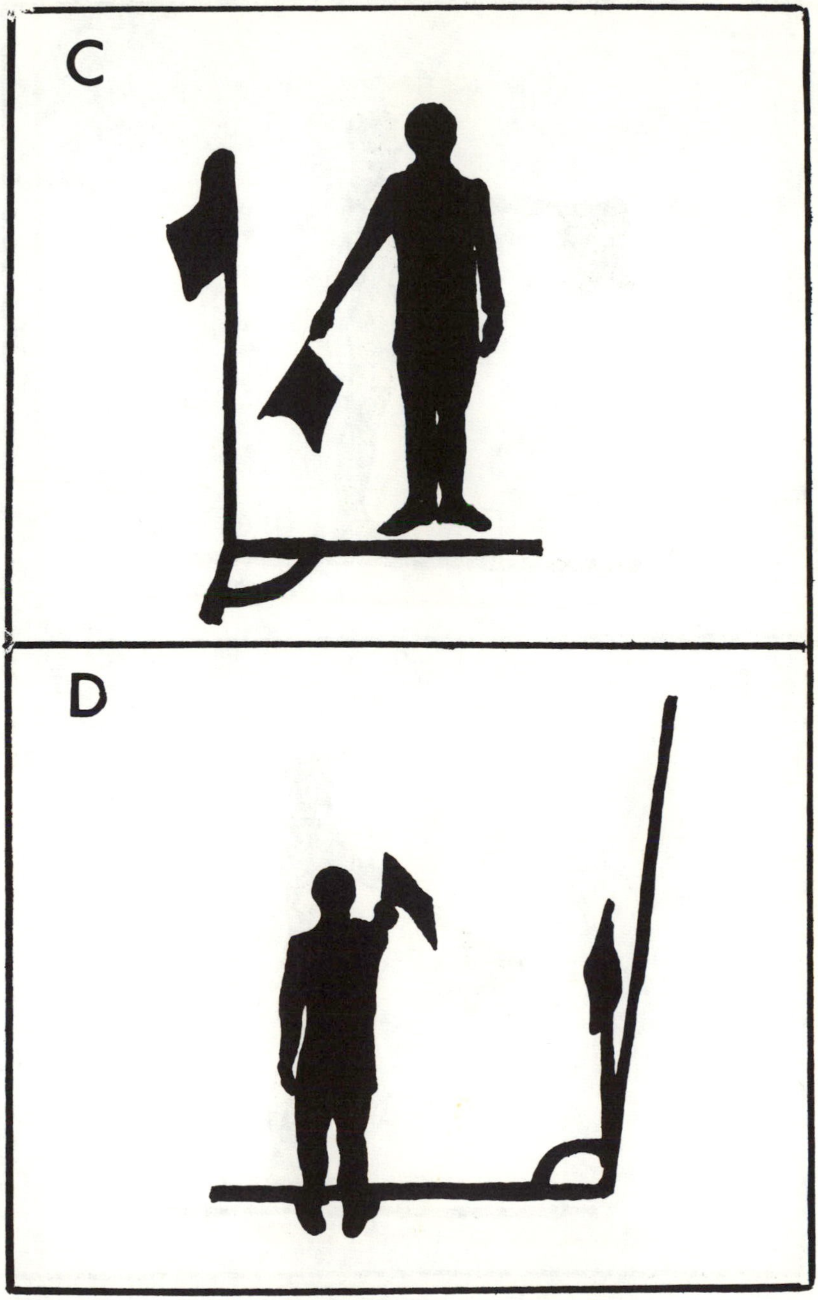
C
D

E

F

G

H
I

J
K

L

M

N

O

P

Q

R

S

T

U

V

W

X
Y

Z

A1

B1

C1

SIGNAL ANSWERS (SOCCER):

A. Stop Play -Offside: Line judge should indicate he/she has seen an offside.
B. Offside Free Kick: When referee stops play, line judge indicates position on far side of the field.
C. Corner Kick: Line judge should point to the nearest corner.
D. Goal Kick: Line judge should point to the goal area.
E. Offside Free Kick: When referee stops play, the line judge indicates position near center of the field.
F. Offside Free Kick: When referee stops play, line judge indicates position on near side of the field.
G. Throw-in: The line judge indicates the direction of the throw-in by bringing the flag up to a 45 degree angle in the direction the throw-in is to be taken. During the taking of the throw-in, the line judge looks for foot faults as outlined in rule 15-1-3. The flag should not be brought across the body. Appropriately, the flag should be switched to the alternate hand.
H. Goal
I. Offside
J. Kicking
K. Tripping
L. Striking
M. Jumping
N. Handling Ball
O. Holding
P. Pushing
Q. Charging Violently Charging-Behind
R. Goalkeeper Carrying Ball
S. Dangerous Play
T. Corner Kick, Penalty Kick or Goal Kick
U. Direct Kick (Points in direction of kick)
V. No Goal
W. Time-out
X. Indirect Kick (Hold until second player touches ball)
Y. Obstruction (Hit the Chest with Palms)
Z. Play On
A1. Dead Ball
B1. Unsportsmanlike Conduct
C1. Start or Restart Game (Circular motion with one arm)

CHAPTER XIV

TENNIS

Considered by many to be a glamour sport, tennis offers championship games that attract prestigious crowds, heavy media coverage and highly paid competitors. Because of this attention, there is a need for highly qualified and well compensated officials.

Tennis was developed in England in the mid-1800s and spread quickly to other countries. It was first introduced to the United States by Mary Ewing Outerbridge, an American sportswoman, in 1874 when she established the first U. S. tennis court.

Most of the world's tennis players are amateurs and play at public courts, private tennis clubs or on the high school and college levels. The International Tennis Federation (ITF) consists of national tennis associations of approximately 100 countries. This federation governs the game of tennis throughout the world. The United States Tennis Association (USTA) governs tennis in the United States for both amateurs and professionals and sponsors tournaments for players from 12 to 75 years of age.

Professional tennis players compete on an international level for more than $12 million dollars in prize money and several earn more than $350,000 a year. The best known professional team tennis tournament is the Davis Cup, which represents the world's men's team championship.

The game of tennis is played with two or four players depending on whether the match is singles or doubles. In most amateur tennis matches, the players officiate their own matches and keep their own score. On the college and professional level, however, many officials may be used. The chief official is the tournament referee and he is responsible for the conduct of the entire tournament. The head official on the court is the chair umpire who announces the score and supervises the line judges. There can be up to 13 line judges stationed at various spots around the court and are responsible for calling balls out and faults on serves.

A primary consideration in being a tennis official is good eyesight, athletic awareness, the ability to accept criticism, and the desire to assist players to play during the match within the rules of the game.

The Umpire's Council was established in 1976 at the District, Sectional and National levels for the expressed purpose of teaching, developing and certifying needed officials. An individual who becomes a member of the USTA in compliance with the certification requirements, may join the United States Council.

The best way to get started in becoming an official is to contact one of the 17 local or regional tennis umpires' groups which are located throughout the country. They can supply you with a manual entitled "A Friend at Court" that details rules and procedures, and provides a test that will gain membership in the U. S. Tennis Association.

If you are interested in becoming a professional tennis official, you will also need to join one of the professional official tennis organizations. The three major ones are:

MEN'S INTERNATIONAL PROFESSIONAL
TENNIS COUNCIL (MIPTC)
-or-
NEW ENGLAND TENNIS UMPIRES
ASSOCIATION (NETUA)
-or-
UMPIRES' DEPT., U.S. TENNIS
ASSOCIATION (USTA)

The above organizations have approved and certified training schools which will expedite your career. If you are interested in acquiring up-to-date information on tennis officiating opportunities, you should contact USTA, 51 East 42nd Street, New York, NY 10017, or call (212) 949-9112.

The Umpires' Council has been established since 1976 at the district, sectional and national levels for the purpose of teaching, developing and certifying tennis officials. Any USTA member who complies with their certification requirements may join the Umpires' Council. the USTA Umpire Committee is responsible for administrating and supervising the Umpires' Council. They prepare and revise the annual membership application procedures and tests for each category of officials. Each sectional and district association designates the Umpire Committee complete with a chairman and vice-chairman. These committees assist the USTA Umpires' Committee with the administration of the Umpires' Council. The sectional and district levels may establish their own certification requirements for non-members of the Umpires' Council.

Certification of officials is performed on an annual basis. Tests and membership applications are available through the district, sectional and USTA chairmen of umpires, and they are responsible for administering and grading tests.

Sectional officials consist of associate umpires, sectional line umpires and sectional chair umpires. USTA officials consist of USTA line umpires, USTA chair umpires and USTA referees. National officials include national line umpires, national chair umpires and national referees.

Sanctioned and approved events include national championships, Davis Cup, Wightman Cup, Division I and II (or equivalent) intercollegiate matches, international professional tournaments, satellite tournaments, tournaments offering $10,000 or more prize money, Junior Davis Cup and Junior Wightman Cup and tournaments with draws of equivalent quality.

General certification requirements: Each official (except a USTA Referee) must attest to having vision of 20/20 either corrected or uncorrected, each official must pass the written test for the appropriate category, each official (except an associate umpire) must successfully complete a USTA approved umpires clinic or school, the approval of the sectional chairman of umpires must be secured for each official's application and an official should meet the certification requirements of serving in more than just the minimum number of tournaments.

Specific certification requirements:

1). An associate umpire must have served in two tournament matches under the supervision of a certified official.

2). A sectional line umpire must have officiated as a line umpire in five matches in tournament play. Credit may be received for matches served as a chair umpire in district high school or state high school championships.

3). Sectional chair umpires must have officiated as a chair umpire in five matches in two tournaments, and may receive credit for matches served as a chair umpire in district high school or state high school championships.

4). USTA line umpires must have officiated as a line umpire in ten matches in two tournaments, five matches must have been certified previously as a sectional official, and must receive satisfactory evaluations as a line umpire.

5). USTA chair umpires must have officiated in 15 matches in three tournaments, ten matches must have been as chair umpire in tournaments at the District championship level or higher, five matches must have been as a line umpire. The USTA chair umpire must have officiated as a chair umpire in at least one major event, must have officiated as a chair umpire in one tournament at the sectional championship level or higher, must have been certified previously as a sectional line or chair umpire and must receive satisfactory evaluations as a chair umpire.

6). USTA referees must have served as a referee in one USTA sanctioned tournament.

7). A national line umpire must submit a physician's report every two years attesting to having 20/20 vision and stating any restrictions and must have officiated in 20 matches in three tournaments at the district championship level or higher, ten matches of which must have been in the capacity of a line umpire. National line umpires must have been certified as a USTA line umpire or USTA chair umpire within the previous two years, and must receive three satisfactory evaluations as a line umpire from an evaluator approved by the USTA umpires committee, plus the USTA chairman of umpires must approve the application.

8). National chair umpires must comply with the two year physical requirements of having 20/20 vision with restrictions noted, must have officiated in 20 matches, 10 of which must have been as a chair umpire in three major events, five matches must have been as a line umpire in major events. National chair umpires must also be certified as a USTA chair umpire within the previous two years, must receive three satisfactory evaluations as a chair umpire from an evaluator approved by the USTA umpires committee, must have successfully completed a USTA approved umpires school during the preceding three years and must have an application approved by the USTA chairman of umpires.

9). National referees must have served as the referee in three tournaments (two of these tournaments must be major events), must have been certified previously as a USTA Referee, must have passed the Referee's test, and must have an application approved by the USTA Chairman of Umpires.

10). Junior Umpires may consist of any persons under the age of eighteen years old. The certification card must indicate junior umpire status.

How to become a tennis official: The first step in the process is to contact your State High School Athletic Association or the National

Federation of State High School Athletic Associations and request an application and official rule book of regulations pertaining to Tennis. At the same time, the **second step** is to request information pertaining to a listing of accredited local agencies or approved class training stations in your geographical area. You should make plans to attend the next open session. The **third step** is to study the materials so that you will be able to pass the written and practical examination. The **fourth step** is to apply for membership in one or more of the appropriate associations. The necessary information can be obtained by asking your State High School Athletic Association, the Federation of State High School Athletic Associations or local agencies for their recommendations. See Appendix A, which is a listing of all the state high school associations throughout the United States.

Applications take approximately two weeks to process. Fees will normally range between $10 and $20.

During this interim, contact your area recreational director(s), your junior high and high school tennis coach, or private clubs and volunteer to observe and/or officiate with these types of community programs, or at the intramural level. Your involvement will provide you with invaluable practical experience.

NOTE: The Chapter on "Getting Started" will provide you with the step-by-step procedure to progress from the amateur level to college level and professional level of sports officiatings.

You may also refer to Appendix E, which is a listing of private officiating schools and accredited college-level officiating courses throughout the United States. Also, in Appendix B you will find a listing of college conferences and other tennis associations throughout the United States.

Appendix C will provide you with professional associations that utilize the majority of professional officials.

Publications and periodicals are located in Appendix D. They will provide the serious individual with additional background and critical information on the sport.

The major manufacturers of sports-related equipment and supplies can be found in Appendix F. Each sport will require its officials to possess a proper uniform and other officiating equipment. These manufacturers can save you a tremendous amount of time and effort in locating exactly the right pieces of equipment.

COMPENSATION: At the high school level, compensation is difficult to come by. This is merely the initial training ground for new officials. At the college level, however, this becomes a different situation. Generous compensation packages are available for qualified officials. For example: in NCAA Men's and Women's Championship (Divisions I, II and III), the referees' salaries range from $200 to $350 plus travel and expenses, and a chair judge's salary can range from $1,000 to $2,500 per tournament.

At the professional levels, an official should have approximately 15 years experience, of which a minimum of 10 years at the college level. MIPTC holds approximately 88 worldwide tournaments each year (which include the Wimbledon, U. S. Open, French Open and Australian Open). Compensation appears to be increasing each year, and the demand for professional officials will be steady for the next several years. At the Men's Open at Longwood for example $13,000 was budgeted to compensate officials. The meet referee is generally responsible for setting the tournament fees. Linesmen received $15 to $25 for each $1^1/_2$ hours of play, and umpires were compensated $20-50 per match.

Other tournaments will hire their own chair umpire directly. An average fee is $750 to $1,000 per week plus meals and lodging.

BASIC QUESTIONS PERTAINING TO TENNIS

1. The following are components of scoring in tennis: a) 15, b) 30, c) 40, d) deuce, and e) love. (T) or (F)
2. A receiver can be awarded a point if the Server serves two consecutive faults. (T) or (F)
3. The service is "let" when the ball served touches the net, strap or band. (T) or (F)
4. The service is a "fault" when the Server misses the ball in attempting to strike it or if the ball served touches a permanent fixture (other than the net, strap or band) before it hits the ground. (T) or (F)
5. The word "foot" means the extremity of the leg below the ankle. (T) or (F)
6. In delivering the service, the Server shall stand alternately behind the right and left courts beginning from the right in every game. (T) or (F)
7. After a fault (if it is the first fault) the Server shall serve again from behind the same half of the court from which he served that fault. (T) or (F)
8. The ball is in play from the moment at which it is delivered in service. Unless a fault or a let has been called. (T) or (F)
9. If a player commits any act which hinders his opponent in making a stroke, then, if this is deliberate, he shall lose the point or if involuntary, the point shall be replayed. (T) or (F)
10. A ball falling on a line is regarded as falling in the court bounded by that line. (T) or (F)

Answers To Tennis Quiz

1. True
2. True
3. True
4. True
5. True
6. True
7. True
8. True
9. True
10. True

CHAPTER XV

GOLF

More than 16 million people in the United States play golf and spend an estimated $600 million a year on golf balls, clubs, shoes and other equipment.

Although golf may have its earliest beginning from the Roman era, the game of golf is credited with having its origin in Scotland and dates back to the pre-1500s. The game has been popular in the United States since the early 1800s.

Golf is played on the amateur and professional level. Golf organizations throughout the world sponsor annual tournaments which are open to both amateurs and professionals. These tournaments are referred to as "open" tournaments. The two best known open tournaments are the British and the United States Opens. Amateurs and professionals also compete in the Masters Tournament held each year at the National Golf Club in Augusta, Georgia. Men's professional golf is regulated by the Professional Golfer's Association (PGA), which sponsors annual tournaments. The PGA was formed in 1916. It also co-sponsors a yearly series of tournaments called the professional tour. These tournaments are held at golf courses throughout the United States and are almost weekly events.

Since 1948, women's golf is governed by the Ladies Professional Golfer's Association (LPGA), which sponsors tournaments for women similar to those given for men.

Amateur only tournaments are held in the United States, Great Britain, Canada and other countries.

Golf is also played on the international level. Teams of two professional golfers from one country play against a two-man team from another country. The best known international tournament is the World Cup match. The United States and Great Britain compete every two years for the Curtis Cup (women's) and the Walker Cup (men's).

As of 1980, professional men golfers compete for purses totalling more than $13 million a year and women $5 million a year.

The average attendance at the PGA tournaments has tripled from the late 1950s to the late 1970s, and millions of people watch PGA and LPGA tournaments on television. The game of golf has become a multi-million dollar business throughout the United States.

The game is played by using various clubs to strike a small ball initially placed on a tee. The player who successfully holes his (or her) ball in the fewest strokes, is the winner. Because there is a high potential for player to illegally move or reposition the ball when unobserved, officials must maintain a sharp eye and be on the lookout for unsportsmanlike play.

Becoming a golf official is not easy. The first step is to contact the United States Golf Association (USGA) for membership. (Address: Golf House, Far Hills, NJ 07931). You must acquire a complete and up to date rule book that is approved by USGA. They will be able to provide relevant information on attending an approved training clinic or school. Also, contact your state high school athletic association or the National Federation of State High School Associations for a copy of their manual pertaining to golf. See Appendix A, which is a listing of all state high school associations throughout the United States. During this interim, contact your area country clubs, recreational directors or physical education instructors with area facilities, and observe and volunteer to officiate with these types of organizations. Your involvement will provide you with invaluable practical experience.

SPECIAL NOTE ON COMPENSATION: The Professional Golfers Association (PGA) does not provide information on salaries or compensation scales, and will not release such information if requested. According to information available, the PGA has ten full time salaried staff rule officials, and compensation is believed to be very generous. If interested in becoming a full time PGA official, contact the PGA-Tours Office at (904) 285-3700.

Most of the workers at the major PGA Tournaments volunteer their services. This is perhaps the only way most officials will be able to acquire practical experience. If you desire to volunteer your services, call the PGA-Tour Volunteer Coordinator at (904) 285-3301.

CHAPTER XVI

VOLLEYBALL

In the United States, volleyball is purely an amateur sport with teams competing on the intramural, high school and college levels. The first U. S. tournaments were held in the 1920s and the first international tournament began by the late 1920s due to growing popularity — hence the need for knowledgeable officials.

Volleyball is a team sport which was invented by William G. Morgan, a physical education instructor for the YMCA in Holyoke, Massachusetts. The game of volleyball is very popular in the United States, Asia and Europe. The International Volleyball Federation sponsors annual tournaments for men's and women's teams. There are more than 120 national members of the federation including the United States and Canada.

Collegiate level volleyball is regulated by the NCAA and championships are held on the Division I, II and III levels.

As of 1964, volleyball has been recognized by the International Olympic Committee as an approved competitive sport. Today, the game can be played either indoors or outside.

There are, however, a long list of specific rules that must be observed in competitive play. For example, the game should be played on a smooth court surface that is 30 x 60 feet with clearly marked lines. Net heights will vary depending upon whether the game is being played by men or women, and the ball must meet specific requirements in terms of size, weight, inflation pressure, casing and structure.

In tournament play, each team will consist of six players stationed in two rows opposite one another. Only the serving teams can score a point. The serve is delivered by the player standing out of bounds in the right rear corner of the court. Movement of players progresses from left to right with the last server taking up a position vacated in the front left position.

A match is won when the first team scores 15 points or has scored the most points after eight minutes of play. The winning team, however, must win by no less than 2 points, and when the lead is less than 2 points, the game proceeds until one team acquires the necessary lead, and this is regardless of the time on the clock. The best of three games will determine the winning match.

Rules governing volleyball were updated in 1983-84, and perhaps one of the most important changes is that an official's judgment is not subject to review. Therefore, schools and universities employing officials may tend to be more selective than in the past.

Collegiate championship games require qualified officials to cover play at the Divisional levels I, II and III.

These officials will usually include a 1st referee, a 2nd referee (or umpire if men's play), two to five linespersons, one scorer, and one or two alternates.

There are three levels (or classes) of referees: Provisional, Regional and National. Each region sets it own rate, but each higher region will pay a higher rate of compensation.

How to become a Volleyball official: The **first step** in the process is to contact your State High School Athletic Association or the National Federation of State High School Athletic Associations and request an application and official rule book of regulations pertaining to Volleyball. At the same time, the **second step** is to request information pertaining to a listing of accredited local agencies or approved class training stations in your geographical area. You should make plans to attend the next open session when it becomes available. The **third step** is to study the materials so that you will be able to pass the written and practical examination. The **fourth step** is to apply for membership in one or more of the appropriate associations. This information can be obtained by asking your State High School Athletic Association, the Federation of State High School Athletic Associations or local agencies for their recommendations. See Appendix A which is a listing of all the state high school associations throughout the United States.

Applications take approximately two weeks to process. Fees will normally range between $10 and $20.

During this interim, contact your area recreational director(s), your junior high and high school volleyball coach, and volunteer to observe and/or officiate with these types of community programs, or at the intramural level. Your involvement will provide you with invaluable practical experience.

NOTE: The chapter on "Getting Started" will provide you with the step-by-step procedure to progress from the amateur level to college level and professional level of sports officiating.

You may also refer to Appendix E, which is a listing of private officiating schools and accredited college-level officiating courses throughout the United States. Also, in Appendix B you will find a listing of college conferences and other volleyball associations throughout the United States.

Publications and periodicals are located in Appendix D. They will provide the serious individual with additional background and critical information.

The major manufacturers of sports-related equipment and supplies can be found in Appendix F. Each sport will require its officials to possess a proper uniform and other officiating equipment. These manufacturers can save you a tremendous amount of time and effort in locating exactly the right piece of equipment.

COMPENSATION: At the recreational level or intramural programs, salaries start at $10 per game. Salaries for junior high school officials start at $15 per official, and high school junior varsity level is $20 per official and varsity level $25-$36 per official based upon two officials.

Salaries for college officials range from $60 to $100 per game and higher depending upon experience, knowledge and rate standing. NOTE: NCAA men's championship Divisions I, II and III officials (one referee and two linesmen) are usually paid $20 for each linesman, plus per diem and travel expenses. Scorers and timers generally range from $25 to $30 based upon experience.

GENERAL QUESTIONS PERTAINING TO VOLLEYBALL

1. A team shall consist of six players to begin the match. (T) or (F)
2. If a team has fewer than six players after the start of the match, it shall continue play. (T) or (F)
3. A playing captain shall be designated by each team, and this is the only player who may communicate with an official during the game. (T) or (F)
4. Teams shall occupy the bench designated by the host team and shall remain there throughout the match. (T) or (F)
5. The official timer shall inspect the timing device and test it to be certain it is in proper working order for use in the match. (T) or (F)
6. A point shall be awarded the serving team when its opponent violates a rule. (T) or (F)
7. A side-out shall be declared when the serving team violates a rule. The ball is given to the serving team's opponents and no points are awarded. (T) or (F)
8. A match is defined when a team has won two out of three. (T) or (F)
9. The net shall be attached from its four corners to walls which are at least six feet from the sideline or to upright standards which are three feet outside the court. (T) or (F)
10. Officials' equipment shall include (a) for the referee, a whistle and (b) for the umpire, a whistle and a record of the lineup. (T) or (F)
11. An umpire and referee should be in uniform and on site no less than 30 minutes before the starting time. (T) or (F)
12. The umpire shall (a) assist the referee in inspecting the playing area and placement of official's table, (b) review the duties and responsibilities with the scorer and timer, and (c) assist with the prematch conference with coaches and captains. (T) or (F)
13. Ten minutes prior to the first game, each team shall submit in writing to the scorer the roster and lineup. (T) or (F)
14. A roster should consist of names and numbers of all players. (T) or (F)
15. A lineup should consist of numbers of the six starting players in serving order. (T) or (F)
16. The first server for each team is the left back player. (T) or (F)
17. A dead ball is one in play, from the moment that contact is made by the server. (T) or (F)
18. A live ball is one declared by an official for any decision temporarily suspending play. (T) or (F)

19. An illegal hit is contact with the ball by a player's body above and including the waist which does not allow the ball to visibly come to a rest even momentarily. (T) or (F)
20. The following are examples of an illegal hit: (a) blocking, (b) setting, and (c) spiking. (T) or (F)

Answers to Volleyball Quiz

1. True
2. True
3. True
4. True
5. True
6. True
7. True
8. True
9. True
10. True
11. True
12. True
13. True
14. True
15. True
16. False
17. False
18. False
19. False
20. False

NATIONAL FEDERATION OF STATE HIGH SCHOOL ASSOCIATIONS VOLLEYBALL OFFICIAL SIGNALS

A volleyball official must know and be able to demonstrate the officially accepted signals. Each of the following drawings represents one specific signal that is utilized during an official game. Attempt to identify (name) the signal depicted in each drawing. Compare your answers to the correct answers located at the end of the chapter.

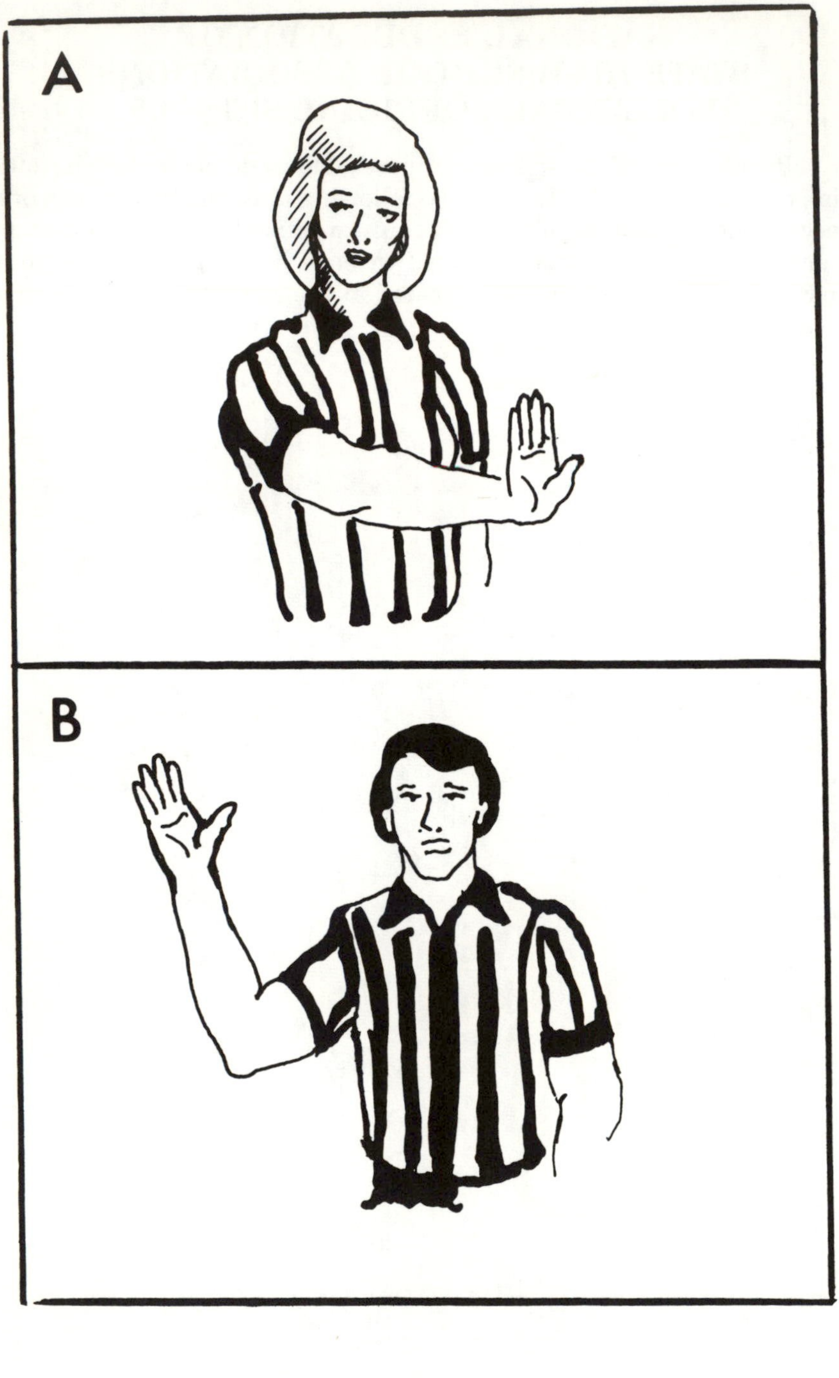
A
B

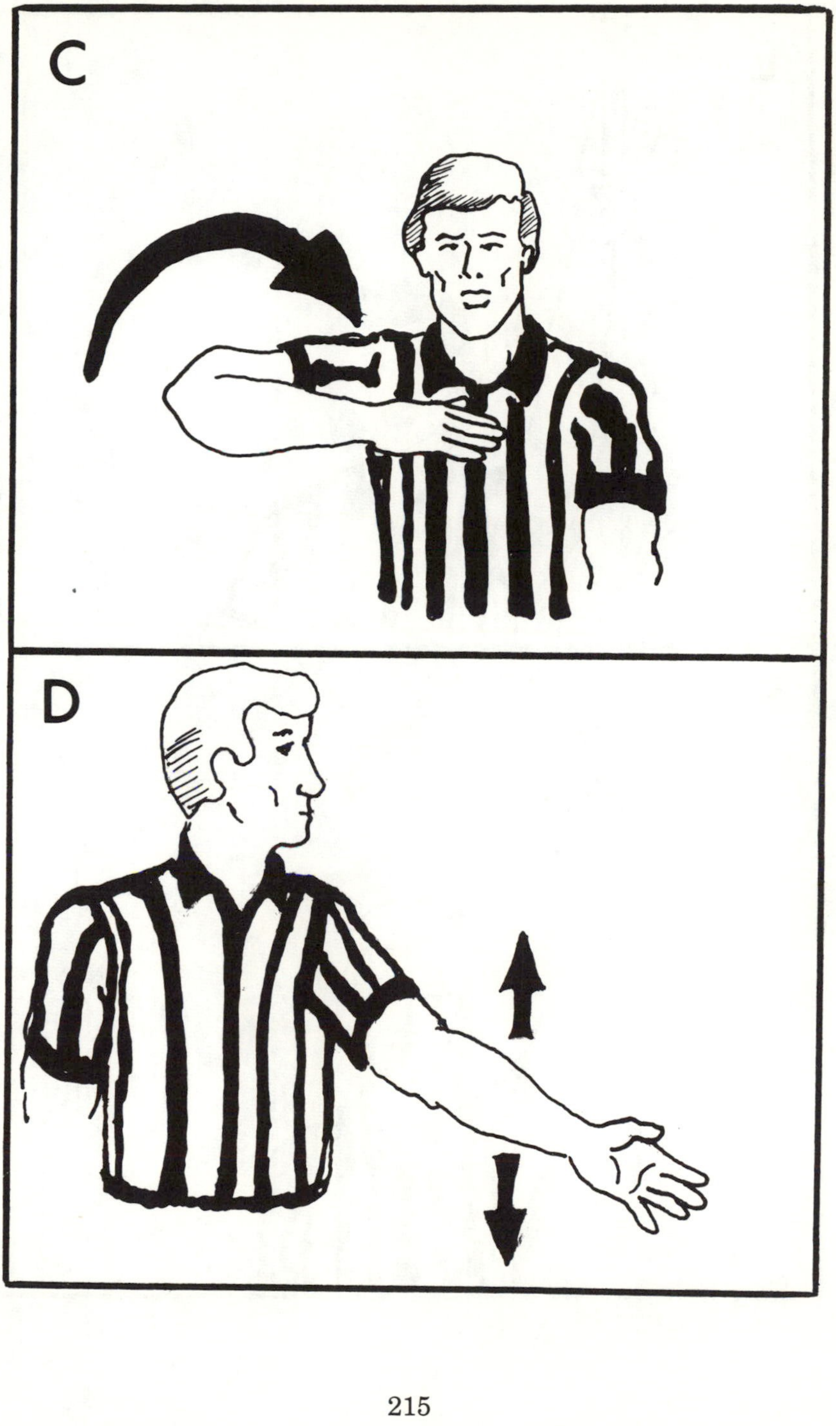
C
D

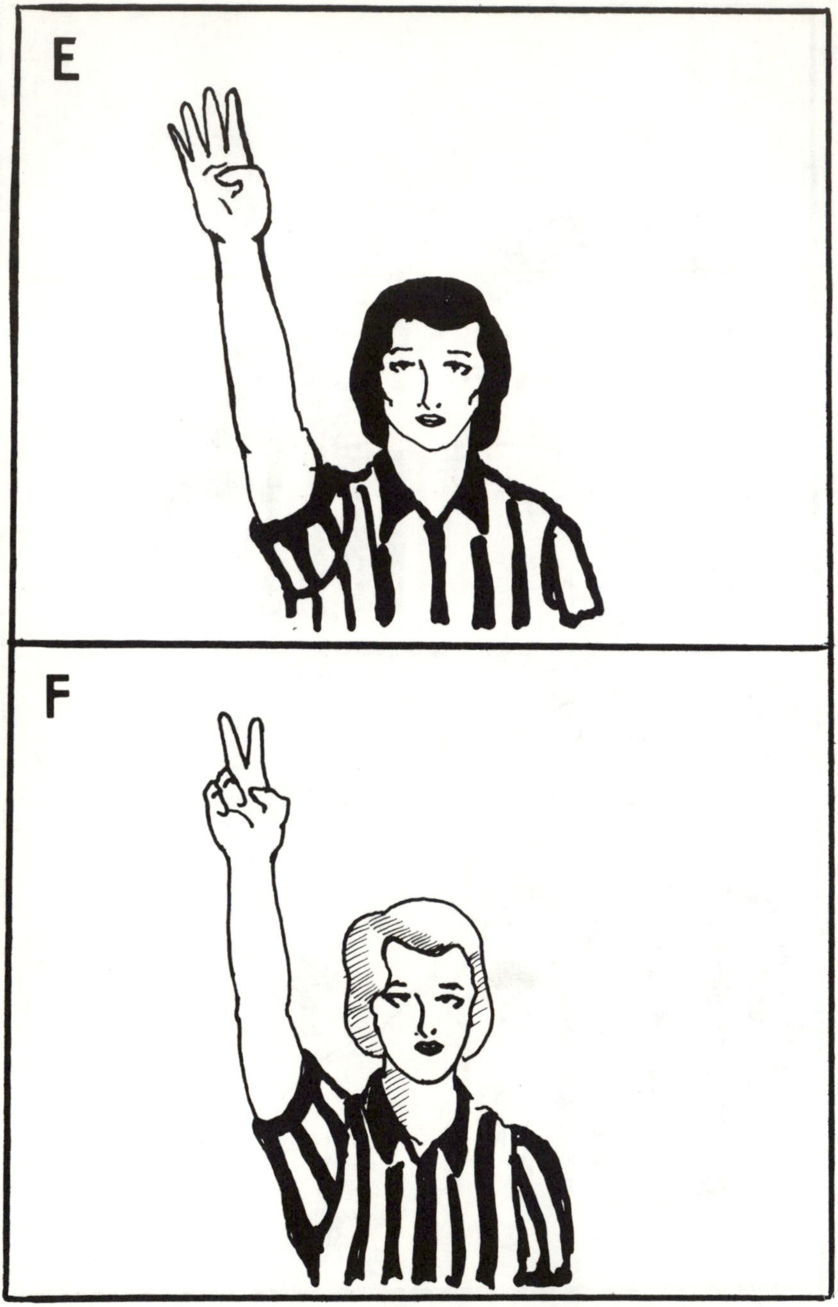
E
F

G

H

I

J

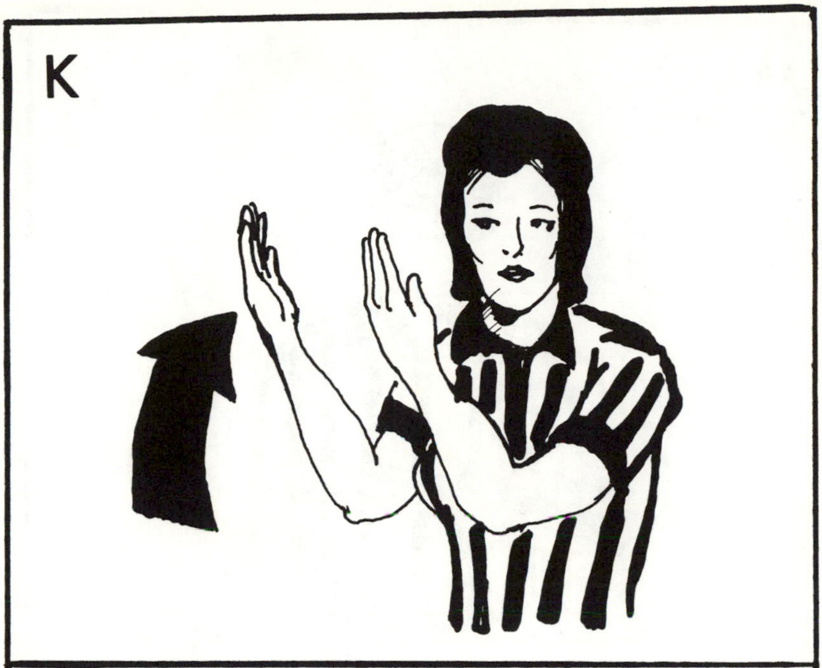
K

L

M

N

O

P

Q

R

S

T

U

V

SIGNAL ANSWERS (Volleyball):

A. Illegal Hit or Serve
B. Delay of Service
C. Over the Net
D. Net Foul
E. Four Hits
F. Double Hit
G. Backline Player Foul
H. Ball Touched
I. Ball Lands In-bounds
J. In-bounds
K. Out-of-Bounds
L. Begin Serve
M. Side-Out
N. Point
O. Replay
P. Substitution
Q. Illegal Substitution
R. Time-Out
S. Unnecessary Delay
T. Unsportsmanlike Conduct
U. Illegal Alignment
V. Foot Foul

CHAPTER XVII

TRACK & FIELD

Annual track and field meets are held on the amateur, local, state, national and international levels. Teams represent elementary schools, high schools, universities and colleges, sports clubs and nations.

The Olympic games in ancient Greece were the earliest known track and field competition. The sport is now governed by the International Amateur Athletic Federation (IAAF) and more than 150 nations belong to the federation.

The National Collegiate Athletic Association (NCAA) sponsors an annual championship meet for member colleges and the NAIA holds similar meets for its members. Meets are also sponsored by the Amateur Athletic Union (AAU) and the United States Track and Field Federation.

Track and field events primarily consist of running, jumping and throwing. Events can be held both outdoors and indoors. Rules set down for most events (be they cross-country, running, pole vaulting, discus throwing, etc.) have been generally established by the International Amateur Athletic Federation (IAAF), the Athletic Congress of the United States of America (TAC-USA) and the Amateur Athletic Union of the United States (AAU).

Track and field events have their foundation as far back as ancient man when tribesmen depended upon running speed, muscle power and throwing accuracy for survival. Starting with Greek Olympic Games (776 BC), most of these events have become formalized throughout the world.

Since 1969, track and field has seen a critical rise in the need for more competent officials. Today, applicants are required to receive appropriate instruction, testing, evaluation and experience to receive certification. The leading active organization in the country today is The Athletic Congress of the United States of America (TAC/USA). The organization provides interested sports officials with a complete and well structured procedure for acquiring acceptance into officiating track and field.

Track and field "meet" officials generally consist of three categories: (1) track officials, (2) field officials and (3) special officials. Each group requires the participation of several officials to perform specific tasks and assignments.

Track Officials	*Field Officials*	*Special Officials*
Referee	Head Field Judge	Walk Judge
Starter	Discus Throw	Distance Run
Head Clerk	Hammer Throw	Wind Gauge
Head Finish	Javelin Throw	Photo Evaluator
Finish Judge	Shot-Put	Official Scorer
Head Timer	High Jump	Official Recorder
Timer	Long Jump	Chronomix Operator
Inspector	Triple Jump	Weights & Measures
Marshall	Pole Vault	

Officials are ranked according to their level of qualifications and experience. These levels (or ranks) consist of Association, National and Master (the highest rank). Those with Association status must serve under the supervision or guidance of a National or Master who will evaluate their performance.

All of the above officials perform their assignments under the direction of the games committee and the meet director. It is the games committee that will determine: meet time schedules, the number of heats required, the number to qualify for the next round of competition, the method of exchanging the baton in relays not run in lanes, the starting height of the crossbar, location of throwing areas, length of spikes and marking material used on all-weather surfaces, the order that contestants take their trials, the time limitation (or number of warm-ups) in the field events, and the time the field events will terminate.

How to become a track & field official: For additional contacts and information on official rule books and regulations pertaining to track & field, contact your State High School Association or the National Federation of State High School Associations for a copy of their current manual. See Appendix A, which is a listing of all the state high school associations throughout the United States. In addition, the International Amateur Athletic Federation (IAAF), the Amateur Athletic Union (AAU) and The Athletic Congress of the United

States (TAC/USA) should also be contacted for membership. (See Appendix D for telephone numbers)

TAC's Official Examination is perhaps one of the most comprehensive evaluation tests administered to track and field officials. TAC will provide you with their complete examination (100 questions in length) plus an answer sheet. To request a TAC Rule Book and Officials Examination, contact:

The Athletic Congress of the United States
Charles M. Ruter, Administrator
P. O. Box 91053
Fern Creek, KY 40291
(502) 239-5258

Applications take approximately two weeks to process. Fees will normally range between $10 and $20.

During this interim, contact your area recreational director(s), your junior high and high school track coaches and observe and/or volunteer to officiate with these types of community programs, or at the intramural level. Your involvement will provide you with invaluable practical experience.

NOTE: The Chapter on "Getting Started" will provide you with the step-by-step procedure to progress from the amateur level to college level and professional level of sports officiating.

You may also refer to Appendix E, which is a listing of private officiating schools and accredited college-level officiating courses throughout the United States. Also, in Appendix B you will find a listing of college conferences and other track and field associations throughout the United States.

Publications and periodicals are located in Appendix D. They will provide the serious individual with additional background and critical information pertaining to track and field.

The major manufacturers of sports-related equipment and supplies can be found in Appendix F. Each sport will require its officials to possess a proper uniform and other officiating equipment. These manufacturers can save you a tremendous amount of time and effort in locating exactly the right piece of equipment.

COMPENSATION: Most track and field positions are filled by volunteers at the lower levels or receive only a stipend. Once an official becomes a member of a state high school association, The Athletic Congress of the United States (TAC/USA), International Amateur Athletic Federation (IAAF) or the Amateur Athletic Union of the United States (AAU), they will be compensated according to structured scales.

At the recreational level or intramural programs, salaries start at $10 per meet. Salaries for junior high school officials start at $22.50 per starter official, and high school (Junior Varsity level) is $25 for the starter official and (Varsity level) $25 to $40 per starter official. When special meets involve invitationals meets, state, regional and district competition, track, field and special officials salaries are increased providing the officials are members in one of the above professional organizations and have acquired a reasonable amount of experience and proficiency.

Salaries for college starter officials will range from $75 to $100 per meet. NCAA Track & Field championships that are broadcast by television, compensation will be higher. Scorers and timers generally range from $20 to $30 based upon experience. The majority of officials will receive travel and expense allowances.

GENERAL QUESTIONS PERTAINING TO TRACK AND FIELD

1. The ________________ shall inspect and measure the track and all courses and takeoffs for the jumps and vaults, throwing circles for the shot and discus.
2. The ________________ and assistants shall keep the grounds free from all persons except officials, contestants and other individuals authorized by the games committee.
3. The ________________ shall keep a record of the contestants, the point winners in each event and complete team scores.
4. The head ________________ ________________ shall have jurisdiction over all judges in the field events, and shall measure, weigh and inspect the implements and apparatus.
5. The head ________________ shall have general supervision over the assistant inspectors and be responsible for placing the inspectors at posts from which they may carry out their responsibilities.
6. The ________________ of ________________ must carefully inventory and arrange all awards before the meet starts.
7. A ________________ is any athlete entered in the meet.
8. To ________________ is to win the right to participate in the next level of competition by meeting certain standards in an earlier race or flight.
9. A ________________ meter track is standard.
10. A ________________ is the course which is marked on the track for a race or that part of a race during which the runner must stay in a prescribed path.
11. An ________________ is a combination of two or more adjoining lanes which are utilized when there or more runners start from the same stagger.
12. The relay ________________ shall not exceed 11.81 in. (30 cm) length.
13. A ________________ is an attempt in a throwing event.
14. A ________________ is a round of trials for a group of contestants in a throwing event.
15. A ________________ ________________ is one which is counted as a trial but which is not measured because of some violation of the rule.
16. The ________________ ________________ may change the order of competition to accommodate those who may be excused to participate in other events.

Answers To Field Hockey Quiz

1. Surveyor
2. Marshall
3. Scorer
4. Field Judge
5. Inspector
6. Custodian, awards
7. Contestant
8. Qualify
9. 400
10. Lane
11. Alley
12. Baton
13. Trial
14. Flight
15. Foul throw
16. Head judge

CHAPTER XVIII

FIELD HOCKEY

Field Hockey is an outdoor sport, played on a closely cut grass or flat dirt surface. As in soccer and football, each team consists of 11 players who use bent sticks to move the ball into the opponent's goal. The game is thought to have originated in Greece. Modern field hockey was established in England about 1875. At the time it was played only by men. By 1889, women in England had formed the All England Women's Hockey Association. In the United States the sport is more popular with women than men.

The game was promoted in the United States by Constance M. K. Applebee of the British College of Physical Education. The United States Field Hockey Association (USFHA) was organized in 1922 and holds national tournaments each year. The International Federation of Women's Hockey Association was formed in 1927 and about 35 countries throughout the world belong.

The game is administered by two officials holding equal jurisdiction over the game, with each official being responsible for one half of the field. The sport is played on a rectangular field, which is clearly marked by white lines to indicate the boundaries, goal lines, side lines and the centerline. For a goal to be scored, which counts one point, the ball must pass over the goal line and between the goal posts and under the crossbar, delivered by a stick.

How to become a field hockey official: The **first step** in the process is to contact your State High School Athletic Association or the National Federation of State High School Athletic Associations and request an application and official rule book of regulations pertaining to field hockey. At the same time, the **second step** is to request information pertaining to a listing of accredited local agencies or approved class training stations in your geographical area. You should make plans to attend the next open session. The **third step** is to study the materials so that you will be able to pass the written and practical examination. The **fourth step** is to apply for membership in one or more of the appropriate associations. This information can be obtained by asking your State High School Athletic Association, the Federation of State High School Athletic Associations or local agencies for their recommendations. See Appendix A, which is a listing of all the state high school associations throughout the United States.

Applications take approximately two weeks to process. Fees will normally range between $10 and $20.

During this interim, contact your area recreational director(s), your junior high and high school field hockey coach, and volunteer to observe and/or officiate with these types of community programs, or at the intramural level. Your involvement will provide you with invaluable practical experience.

NOTE: The Chapter on "Getting started" will provide you with the step-by-step procedure to progress from the amateur level to college level and professional level of sports officiating.

You may also refer to Appendix E, which is a listing of private officiating schools and accredited college-level officiating courses throughout the United States. Also, in Appendix B you will find a listing of college conferences and other field hockey associations throughout the United States.

Publications and periodicals are located in Appendix D. They will provide the serious individual with additional background and critical information.

The major manufacturers of sports-related equipment and supplies can be found in Appendix F. Each sport will require its officials to possess a proper uniform and other officiating equipment. These manufacturers can save you a tremendous amount of time and effort in locating exactly the right piece of equipment.

COMPENSATION: At the junior high and recreational levels, compensation ranges up to $17.50 for each official; at the high school level, junior varsity and varsity officials range up to $30 per official. At the college level and above, compensation starts at $60 to $75 plus mileage per official with alternates being allotted $30 to $35.

Compensation for scorers and timers at the amateur level starts at $10 to $25, and at the college level, $25 and above depending upon experience.

GENERAL QUESTIONS PERTAINING TO FIELD HOCKEY

1. "Bully" is a term describing a method used by two opposing players to start or re-start the game. (T) or (F)
2. "Free Hit" is a means of putting the ball in play by any player following a foul by an opponent. Any legal stroke is allowed. (T) or (F)
3. Legal strokes in field hockey include flick, hit, drive, scoop or push. (T) or (F)
4. Penalty stroke is a shot on the goal taken by any attacker against the goalkeeper from the penalty mark 20 yards in front of the center of the goal. (T) or (F)
5. A "Push-In" is the method for putting the ball in play after it has gone out of bounds. (T) or (F)
6. An "Obstruction" occurs when a player places any part of a player's body or stick between the ball and an opponent who is attempting to play the ball. (T) or (F)
7. "Off-Side" occurs when a player is in advance of the ball in the opponent's half of the field and there are fewer than two opponents between the player and the goal-line at the time the ball is hit. (T) or (F)
8. Stick interference occurs when a player hits, holds, hooks, slashes or strikes another opponent's stick. (T) or (F)
9. "Undercutting" is propelling the ball with a hard hit on the underside, causing the ball to be delivered in an acceptable manner. (T) or (F)
10. The clock-running time for a game shall be ninety minutes played in two equal halves. (T) or (F)
11. The clock shall be started immediately upon the official's whistle prior to the pass-back at the beginning of each half. (T) or (F)
12. The game clock shall be stopped by the official's signal for (a) injury to a player or official, (b) penalty strokes, (c) awarding a penalty corner at the opposite end of the field, (d) disqualification of a player, and (e) any reason as determined by the official which interferes with the continuous flow of play. (T) or (F)
13. "Fouls" include the following: (a) advancing, (b) sticks, (c) obstruction, (d) dangerous kicking by goalkeeper, and (e) charging, pushing and/or striking another opponent. (T) or (F)
14. It is legal for a goalkeeper to place tow marks on the ground three feet in front of the goal cage. (T) or (F)

15. During a tournament, an official does not have a say on which ball is to be used. (T) or (F)
16. It is legal for the goalkeeper to wear a softball helmet with a wire mask for protection. (T) or (F)
17. Approximately 15 minutes prior to the start of the game, the officials shall examine the following: (a) the field, (b) the goal cages, nets and posts, (c) striking circles and other field markings, and (e) proper placement of team benches as well as the officials' table. (T) or (F)
18. The officials' conference shall include the following: (a) discussion of the area of field to be played on, (b) administration involving penalty strokes, and (c) other areas of cooperation. (T) or (F)
19. Timers and scorers should have a conference to discuss (a) assignments, and (b) check both clocks. (T) or (F)
20. During a penalty corner, the defending team has five players behind its goal line. (T) or (F)

Answers To Field Hockey Quiz

1. True
2. True
3. True
4. False
5. True
6. True
7. True
8. True
9. False
10. False
11. True
12. True
13. True
14. False
15. False
16. False
17. True
18. True
19. True
20. True

NATIONAL FEDERATION OF STATE HIGH SCHOOL ASSOCIATIONS FIELD HOCKEY OFFICIAL SIGNALS

A field hockey official must know and be able to demonstrate the officially accepted signals. Each of the following drawings represents one specific signal that is utilized during an official game. Attempt to identify (name) the signal depicted in each drawing. Compare your answers to the correct answers located at the end of the chapter.

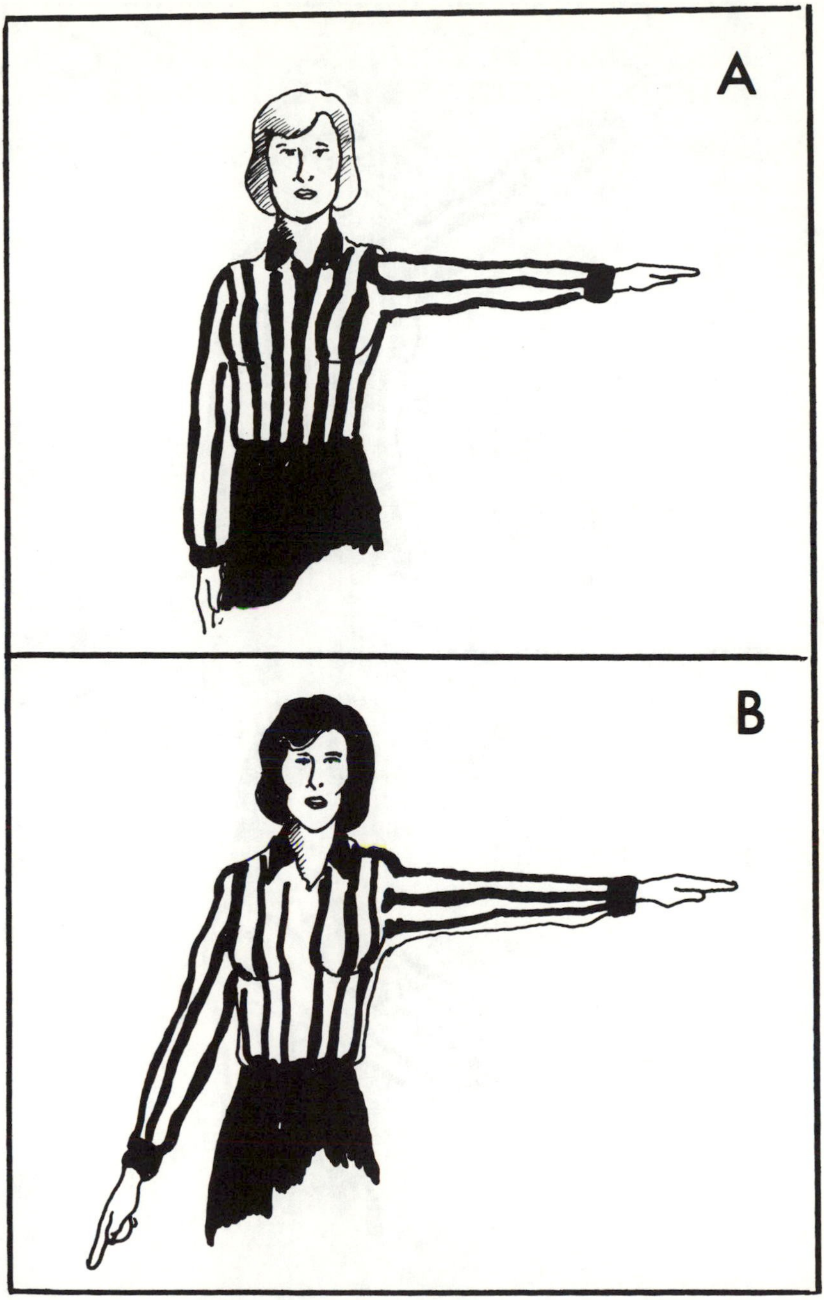
A
B

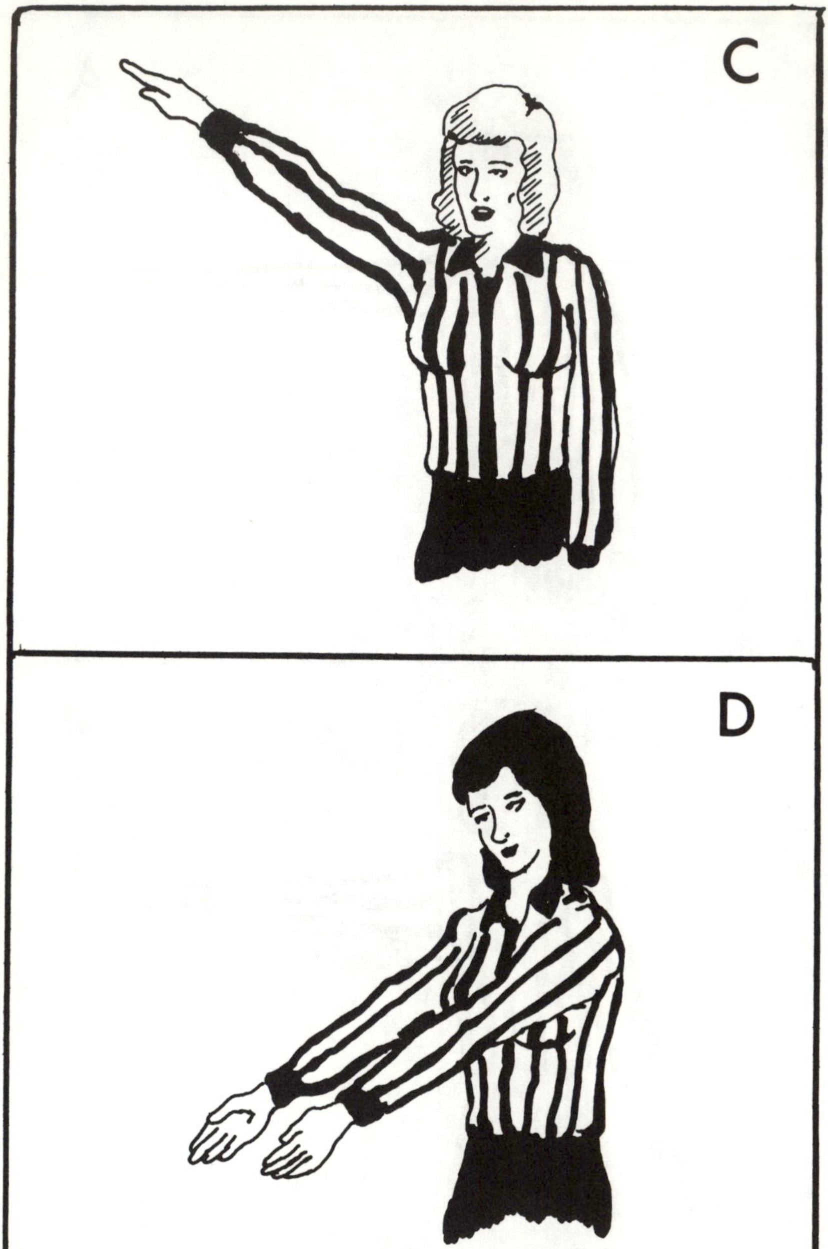
C
D

E

F

G
H

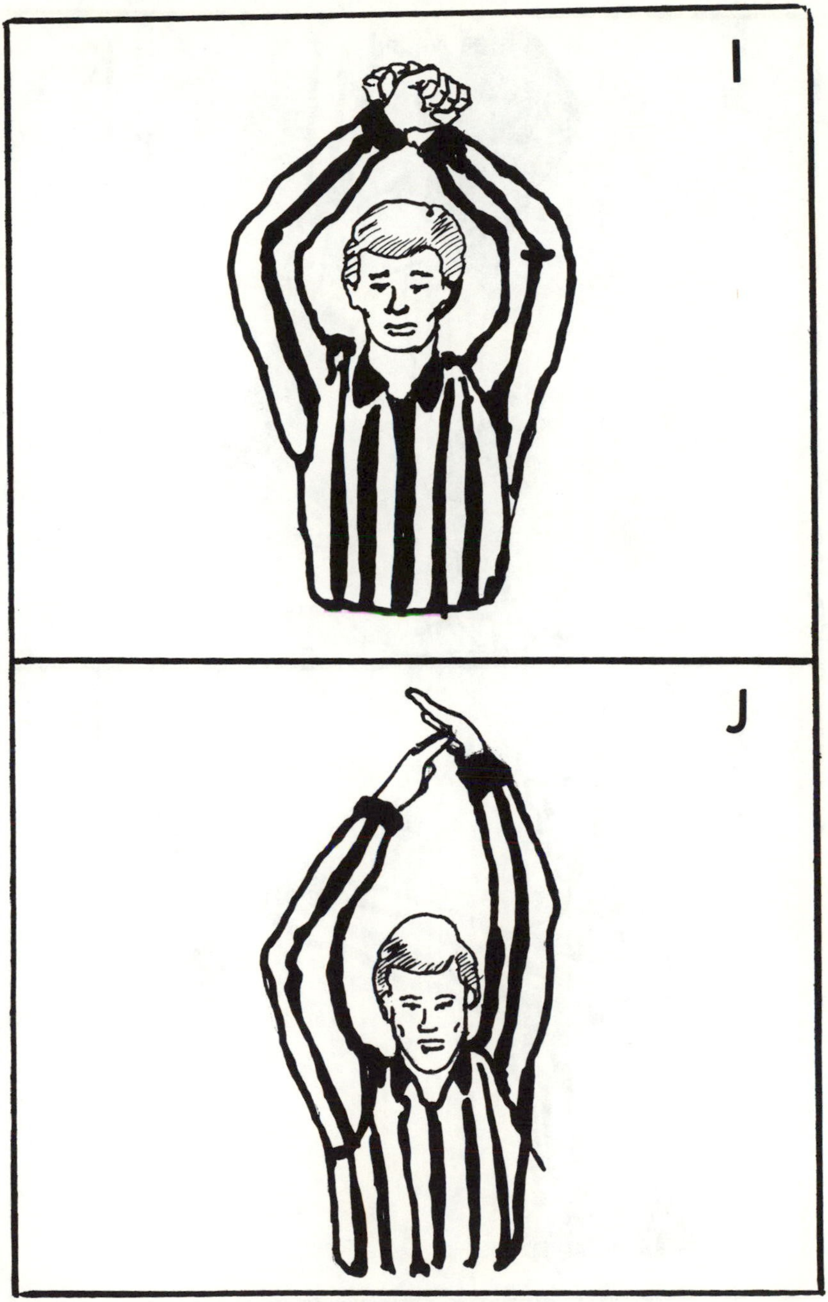
I
J

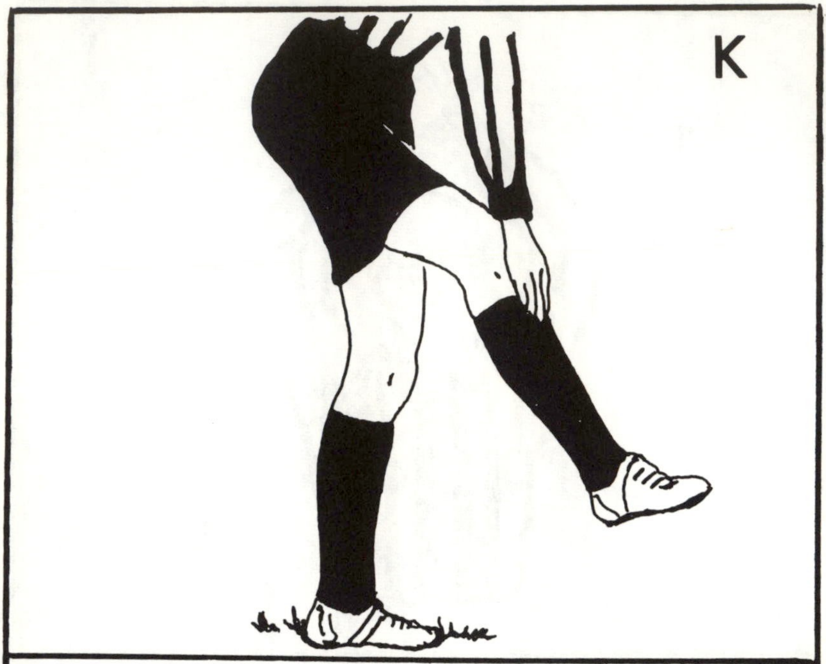
K

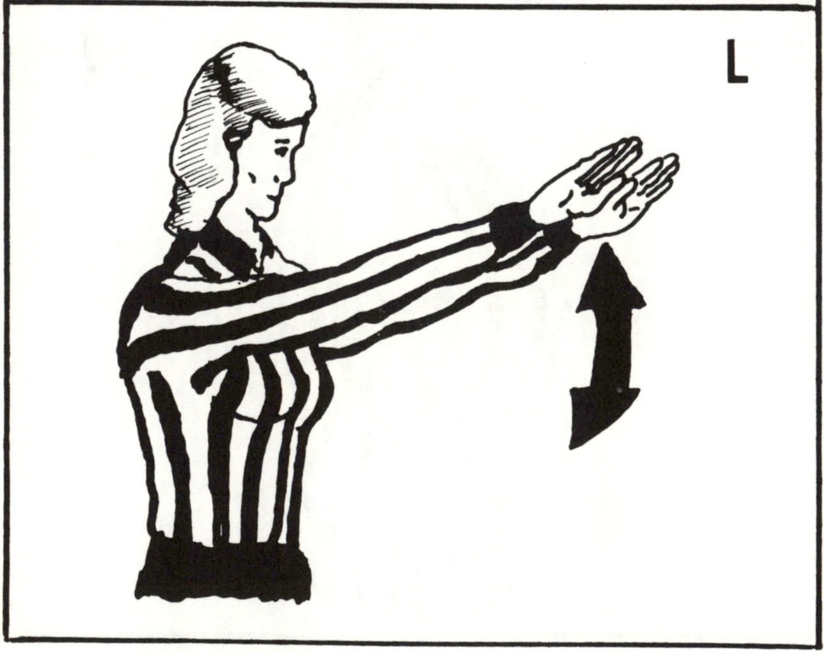
L

M

N

O

P

Q

R

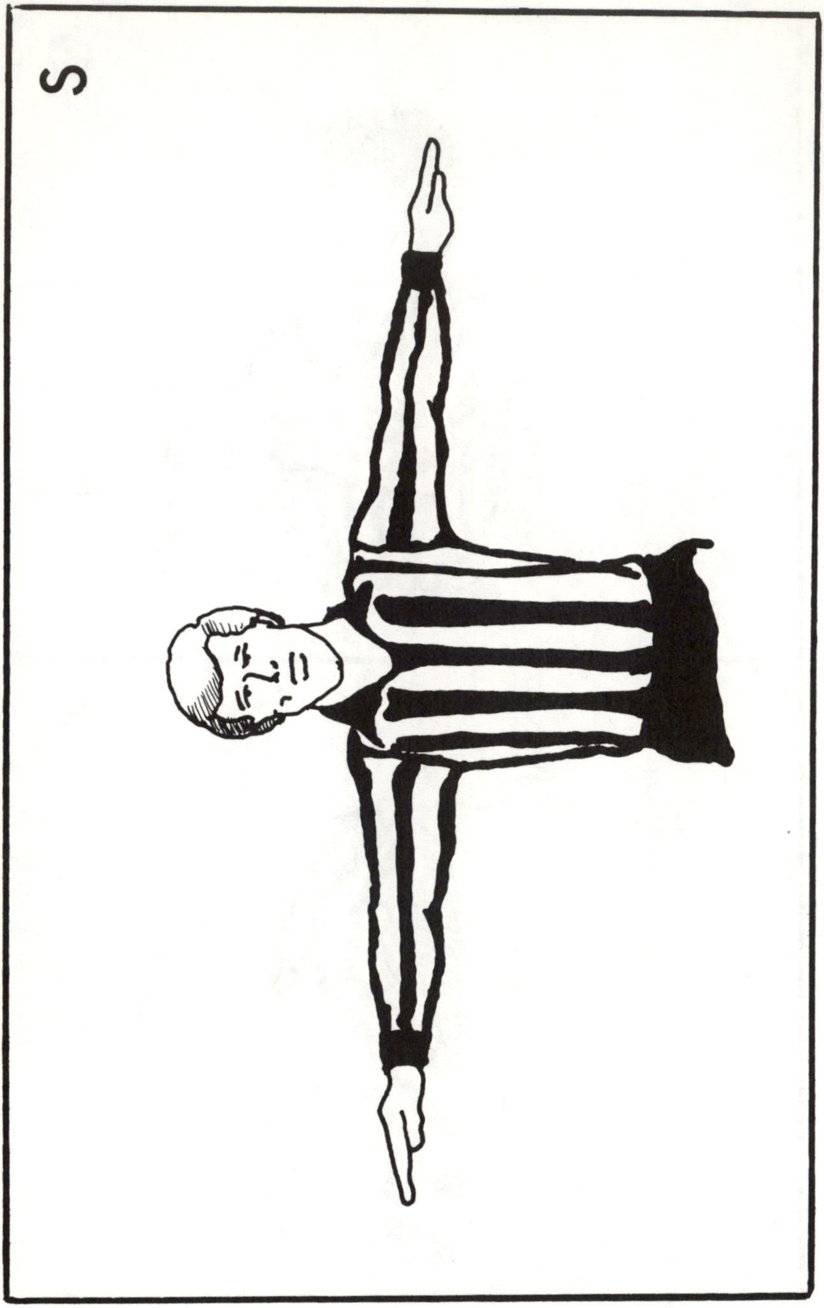
S

SIGNAL ANSWERS (Field Hockey):

A. Free Hit
B. Push-in
C. Long Hit
D. Penalty Corner
E. Goal Scored
F. Goal Scored
G. Offside
H. Third Party Obstruction
I. Time Out
J. Time Out
K. Advancing
L. Penalty Stroke
M. Penalty Stroke
N. Penalty Stroke
O. Bully
P. Obstruction
Q. Stick Interference
R. Dangerous use of Stick
S. 16-Yard Hit

CHAPTER XIX

GYMNASTICS

Gymnastic exercises require numerous daring and extremely difficult coordinated maneuvers, and involve the use of various pieces of apparatus. Today, the sport is well structured and defined for both women and men. The first modern gymnastics equipment was built in the early 1800s by a German school teacher, Friedrich Jahn. From that time, the popularity of gymnastics has increased and in 1896 gymnastics became a recognized Olympic sport.

Amateur competition in the United States is governed by the United States Gymnastics Federation (USGF). This organization is a member of the International Gymnastics Federation (IGF), which governs international competitions such as the Olympics, the Pan-American Games, the World Games and the World University Games.

In the United States many states hold competitions on the high school level. The National Collegiate Athletic Association (NCAA), National Association of Intercollegiate Athletics (NAIA) and the National Junior College Athletic Association (NJCAA) sponsors men's regional and national championships on the collegiate level.

The United States uses one of four (or a combination of) structured gymnastic systems: Danish, Swedish, German and American. Each of these systems has its own special characteristics. For example, Danish gymnastics consists of a continuous group drill that stresses flexibility, balance, agility and endurance. Swedish gymnastics emphasizes good posture and fixed positions that utilizes such equipment as balance beams, stall bars, benches and long horses. German gymnastics incorporates a wider variety of equipment such as parallel bars, ropes, rings, bucks and horizontal bars. Naturally, the American gymnastic system combines most of the European features plus adding a few of its own such as tumbling, trampoline, obstacle courses, steeplechases and indoor track.

Competitive gymnastics is probably one of the most difficult sports to officiate well because there are questions as to what constitutes good form, good posture and dynamic execution. Sometimes, there is a fine line between what is more difficult than another to perform. Judging the degree of difficulty requires an educated eye and a thorough knowledge of the exercises.

Judging this type of competitive sport will usually require anywhere from two to 24 officials depending upon the stature of the event. Local gymnastic events utilize two officials. At the Olympics, four or more officials are utilized for each competitive event. Major events include floor exercise, pommel horse, rings, vaulting, parallel bars and horizontal bar.

Becoming a gymnastics official will take a serious commitment. If you are a hard worker and love the sport of gymnastics, this goal can be accomplished. For all events the judges shall award (using a scale of 10), a 10 for a perfect routine. When four judges are being used for an event, the scorer shall note on the score sheets the marks from each judge and then eliminate the highest and lowest marks, using the average of the two intermediate scores for the evaluation of the performance.

How to become a gymnastics official: The **first step** in the process is to contact your State High School Athletic Association or the National Federation of State High School Athletic Associations and request an application and official rule book of regulations pertaining to gymnastics. At the same time, the **second step** is to request information pertaining to a listing of accredited local agencies or approved class training stations in your geographical area. You should make plans to attend the next open session. The **third step** is to study the materials so that you will be able to pass the written and practical examination. The **fourth step** is to apply for membership in one or more of the appropriate associations. This information can be obtained by asking your State High School Athletic Association, the Federation of State High School Athletic Associations or local agencies for their recommendations. See Appendix A, which is a listing of all the state high school associations throughout the United States.

Applications take approximately two weeks to process. Fees will normally range between $10 and $20.

During this interim, contact your area recreational director(s), your junior high and high school gymnastics coach, and volunteer to observe and/or officiate with these types of community programs, or at the intramural level. Your involvement will provide you with invaluable practical experience.

NOTE: The Chapter on "Getting Started" will provide you with the step-by-step procedure to progress from the amateur level to college level and professional level of sports officiatings.

You may also refer to Appendix E, which is a listing of private officiating schools and accredited college-level officiating courses throughout the United States. Also, in Appendix B you will find a listing of college conferences and other gymnastics associations throughout the United States.

For additional contacts and information on official rule books and regulations pertaining to gymnastics, contact your State High School Association or the National Federation of State High School Associations for a copy of their current manual. See Appendix A, which is a listing of all the state high school athletic associations throughout the United States.

In order to officiate at the top amateur gymnastic tournaments, major college competitions and the Junior or Senior Olympics you should be a member of the U. S. Gymnastics Federation (USGF), Merchants Plaza, Suite 1144E, 101 West Washington Street, Indianapolis, IN 46204 (317) 638-8743.

COMPENSATION: At the recreational level or intramural programs, salaries range from $10 to $20 per meet. Salaries for junior high school officials start at $23 to $25 per official (with two officials being used), and high school the range is $38 to $41 per official per meet. When the event is locally televised, officials' fee compensation is typically as follows: announcer official $150, judges $100 and statistician $50.

Salaries for college officials (Division I and II) range from $80 to $100 per first day meet and $40 for each additional day, depending upon experience, knowledge and rate standing, plus 50 cents per mile when the event is more than 200 miles away and per diem expenses. Statisticians, scorers and timers will generally range from $20 to $30 per meet. A two-day event utilizes nine judges the first day and five judges for the second day.

DEFINITION QUESTIONS ON GYMNASTICS

1. Any forward motion toward the long horse that is either stopped or which does not result in a vault is called a ________________.
2. Those limitations indicating size, width, thickness, heights, stress and other pertinent information related to the apparatus is defined as ________________.
3. Any individual designated by the school with the responsibilities of directing its team is called a ________________.
4. The types of skills performed and how they are combined are called ________________.
5. A ________________ is the highest point of a vaulting board.
6. ________________ is a predetermined value of a particular gymnastic skill.
7. The ________________ is the final skill of value used by the gymnast and completes a routine.
8. The name of a particular piece of apparatus which is contested in a gymnastic meet is called ________________.
9. ________________ is the manner in which the gymnast performs his/her routine, taking into consideration both form and techniques.
10. The complete set of skills or routines performed by the gymnast is known as an ________________.
11. ________________ is a point in an exercise in which a gymnast unintentionally stops or alters the rhythm.
12. ________________ is a static position held for two seconds.
13. ________________ is the first skill performed in a routine.
14. ________________ is the person responsible for recording individual gymnast's scores and computing team scores.
15. ________________ is any individual who is in position to aid the gymnast during the exercise.

Answers To Gymnastics Quiz

1. balk
2. apparatus specifications
3. coach
4. combination
5. crown
6. difficulty
7. dismount
8. event
9. execution
10. exercise
11. break
12. hold
13. mount
14. scorer
15. spotter

CHAPTER XX

THE OLYMPICS

Held every four years, the Olympic Games present amateur athletes of many nations competing in a wide variety of sports. The Olympics are divided into the Winter and Summer games, which are held in the same calendar year.

The location of the Olympics is determined by the International Olympic Committee, headquartered in Lausanne, Switzerland. The games are held in a different city each time.

As of 1967, there were 123 nations with National Olympic Committees and in 1984, 144 countries participated in the Summer Olympics in Los Angeles, California.

For a sport to gain official Olympic recognition, it must be played in at least 25 countries. There are seven winter sports with such recognition and 26 summer sports.

As previously stated, the games are governed by the International Olympic Committee. However, the National Committees are responsible for all matters relating to the Olympics in their respective countries. The United States Olympic Committee appoints games committees to oversee special Olympic try-outs. These try-outs are to determine the final composition of the American team.

Often overlooked, but none the less rewarding, are opportunities to participate in officiating at the Olympic level. Competition at this level is perhaps the most competitive. Not every country participating will have an official from its nation officiating each event. Also, only one official from a country is utilized per event. The selection process is extremely demanding. Just as the athletes are thought to be the best their nations have to offer, so are the officials.

As a general rule, you will need a measurable amount of credible experience. The majority of this experience would have to be at the collegiate level and above. Experience officiating national Olympic try-outs would be a bonus to the potential International Olympic official.

If you are selected for an officiating position with the Olympics, the compensation packages are generous in terms of pay, travel expenses and accommodations. Also, each official receives a commemorative Olympic medal.

How to become an Olympic official: Contact the **United States Olympic Committee** located at 1750 East Boulder Street, Colorado Springs, CO 80909, telephone: (303) 632-5551. Under this organization you will find a family of amateur sports organizations that prepare, administrate and participate in Olympic competition — hence the need for qualified officials. The following contacts listed on the following pages will provide individuals with officiating experience with invaluable leads to obtain employment as an Olympic official. Membership in the appropriate association(s) is strongly advised.

U.S. OLYMPIC TRAINING CENTER, 1776 East Boulder Street, Colorado Springs, CO 80909 (303) 578-4500

U.S. OLYMPIC TRAINING CENTER, 122 Main Street, P.O. Box 470, Lake Placid, NY 12946 (518)523-2600

LOS ANGELES OLYMPIC ORGANIZING COMMITTEE, Los Angeles, CA 90084 (213) 305-1984

THE ATHLETICS CONGRESS (TAC), (Track & Field) P.O. Box 120, Indianapolis, IN 46206 (317) 638-9155

NATIONAL ARCHERY ASSOCIATION (NAA), 1750 East Boulder street, Colorado Springs, CO 80909 (303) 578-4576

U.S. BASEBALL FEDERATION (USBF), 4 Gregory Drive, Hamilton Square, NJ 08690 (609) 586-2381

AMATEUR BASKETBALL ASSOCIATION OF THE UNITED STATES (ABAUSA), 1750 East Boulder Street, Colorado Springs, CO 80909 (303) 632-7687

U.S. BIATHLON ASSOCIATION, Adjutant General's Office, Camp Johnson, Bldg 5, Winooski, VT 05404 (802) 655-0270, Ext. 22

U.S. BOBSLED & SKELETON ASSOCIATION, P.O. Box 828, Lake Placid, NY 12946 (518) 523-1842

USA AMATEUR BOXING FEDERATION (USA/ABF), 1750 East Boulder Street, Colorado Springs, CO 80909 (303) 578-4506

AMERICAN CANOE ASSOCIATION (ACA), P.O. Box 248, Lorton, VA 22079 (703) 550-7523

U.S. CYCLING FEDERATION (USCF), 1750 East Boulder Street, Colorado Springs, CO 80909 (303) 578-4581

U.S.A. DIVING, INC. (USD), 901 West New York Street, Indianapolis, IN 46202 (317) 634-3040

AMERICAN HORSE SHOWS ASSOCIATION (AHSA), 598 Madison Avenue, New York, NY 10022

U.S. EQUESTRIAN TEAM (USET), 527 Madison Avenue, New York, NY 10022 (212) 753-1750

U.S. FENCING ASSOCIATION (USFA), 1750 East Boulder Street, Colorado Springs, CO 80909 (303) 578-4511

U.S. FIELD HOCKEY ASSOCIATION (USFHA), (Women) 1750 East Boulder Street, Colorado Springs, CO 80909 (303) 578-4567

FIELD HOCKEY ASSOCIATION OF AMERICA (FHAA), (Men) 1750 East Boulder Street, Colorado Springs, CO 80909 (303) 578-4587

U.S. FIGURE SKATING ASSOCIATION (USFSA), 20 First Street, Colorado Springs, CO 80906 (303) 635-5200

U.S. GYMNASTICS FEDERATION (USGF), Merchants Plaza, Suite 1144E, 101 W. Washington St., Indianapolis, IN 46204 (317) 638-8743

AMATEUR HOCKEY ASSOCIATION OF THE UNITED STATES (AHAUS), 2997 Broadmoor Valley Road, Colorado Springs, CO 80906 (303) 576-4990

UNITED STATES JUDO, INC. (USJ), P.O. Box 637, El Paso, TX 79944 (915) 541-7393

U.S. LUGE ASSOCIATION (USLA), Box 651, One Wilmington Rd., Lake Placid, NY 12946 (518) 523-2071

U.S. MODERN PENTATHLON ASSOCIATION, INC & U.S. MODERN PENTATHLON TRAINING CENTER, Ft. Sam Houston, TX 78234 (512) 221-4732

U.S. AMATEUR CONFEDERATION OF ROLLER SKATING, P.O. Box 83067, Lincoln, NE 68501 (402) 483-7551

U.S. ROWING ASSOCIATION (USRA), #4 Boathouse Row, Philadelphia, PA 19130 (215) 769-2068

NATIONAL RIFLE ASSOCIATION (NRA), 1600 Rhode Island Avenue, NW, Washington, D.C. 20036 (202) 828-6255

U.S. SKI ASSOCIATION (USSA), 1750 East Boulder Street, Colorado Springs, CO 80909 (303) 578-4572

U.S. SKI TEAM (USST), P.O. Box 100, Park City, UT 84060 (801) 649-9090

U.S. SOCCER FEDERATION (USSF), 350 Fifth Avenue, 4010, New York, NY 10118 (212) 736-0915

AMATEUR SOFTBALL ASSOCIATION (ASA), 2801 NE 50th Street, Oklahoma City, OK 73111 (405) 424-5266

U.S. INTERNATIONAL SPEEDSKATING ASSOCIATION (USISA), Beggs Isle, Oconomowoc, WI 53066 (414) 567-6051

U.S. SWIMMING, INC (USS), 1750 East Boulder Street, Colorado Springs, CO 80909 (303) 578-4578

U.S. SYNCHRONIZED SWIMMING (USSS), 901 West New York Street, Indianapolis, IN 46202 (317) 633-2000

U.S. TABLE TENNIS ASSOCIATION (USTTA), 1750 East Boulder Street, Colorado Springs, CO 80909 (303) 578-4583

U.S. TEAM HANDBALL FEDERATION (USTHF), 1750 East Boulder Street, Colorado Springs, CO 80909 (303) 578-4582

U.S. TENNIS ASSOCIATION (USTA), 51 East 42nd Street, New York, NY 10017 (212) 949-9112

U.S. VOLLEYBALL ASSOCIATION (USVBA), 1750 East Boulder Street, Colorado Springs, CO 80909 (303) 632-5551, Ext. 3312

UNITED STATES WATER POLO (USWP), 1750 East Boulder Street, Colorado Springs, CO 80909 (303) 578-4549

U.S. WEIGHTLIFTING FEDERATION (USWF), 1750 East Boulder Street, Colorado Springs, CO 80909 (303) 578-4508

U.S.A. WRESTLING, 405 West Hall of Fame Avenue, Stillwater, OK 74074 (405) 377-5242

U.S. YACHT RACING UNION (USYRU), P.O. Box 209, Newport, RI 02840 (401) 849-5200

MULTI-SPORT ORGANIZATIONS

NATIONAL COLLEGIATE ATHLETIC ASSOCIATION (NCAA), P.O. Box 1906, Shawnee Mission, KS 66222 (913) 384-3220

NATIONAL ASSOCIATION OF INTERCOLLEGIATE ATHLETICS (NAIA), 1221 Baltimore, Kansas City, MO 64105 (816) 842-5050

NATIONAL JUNIOR COLLEGE ATHLETIC ASSOCIATION (NJCAA) P.O. Box 1586, Hutchinson, KS 67501 (316) 663-5445

AMATEUR ATHLETIC UNION (AAU), 3400 West 86th Street, Indianapolis, IN 46268 (317) 872-2900

NATIONAL FEDERATION OF STATE HIGH SCHOOL ASSOCIATIONS (NFSHSA), P.O. Box 20626, Kansas City, MO 64195 (816) 464-5400

YMCA OF THE USA, 101 North Wacker Drive, Chicago, IL 60606 (312) 977-0031

NATIONAL WHEELCHAIR ATHLETIC ASSOCIATION, 2107 Templeton Gap Road, Suite C, Colorado Springs, CO 80907 (303) 632-0698

CHAPTER XXI

STATISTICIANS – SCORERS & TIMERS

Often overlooked by sports fans and participants alike are the generally unseen officials who monitor and maintain the contest records, time and score. These officials are used in almost every event, and assist field or visible officials such as referees, judges and umpires in the execution of their duties.

How to become a minor official: For additional contacts and information on official rule books and regulations pertaining to scorekeepers, timers and statisticians, contact your State High School Athletic Association or the National Federation of State High School Athletic Associations for copies of their current scorebooks pertaining to all your areas of interest. See Appendix A, which is a listing of all the state high school associations throughout the United States.

Applications take approximately two weeks to process. Fees normally range less than $10.

You should request from the state and national high school associations their listing of any accredited courses and teaching/instructional facilities that may be applicable for certification.

During this interim, contact your area recreational director(s) or the physical education instructor(s) with area facilities, and volunteer to work with these types of community programs, or at the intramural level. Your involvement will provide you with invaluable practical experience.

NOTE: The Chapter on "Getting Started" will provide you with the step-by-step procedure to progress from the amateur level to college level and professional level of sports officiatings. For example, If you are interested in becoming a statistician, scorer or timekeeper in amateur baseball/softball you should become a member of a) Scorekeepers Association, 2801 Northeast 50th Street, Oklahoma City, OK 73111, and b) The National Association of Leagues, Umpires &

Scorers, Box 1420, Witchita, KS 67201. For other minor officiating interests, see Appendix B and C. Here, you will find a listing of amateur, college and professional associations that utilize minor officials throughout the United States pertaining to your specific area of interest.

You should seriously consider joining one or more of these organizations to acquire official recognition. For opportunities pertaining to statisticians, scorers and timers, contact the NCAA, NAIA and CFA at the college level, and for opportunities at the professional level contact the NFL, USFL, NBA, AL, NL, etc. Each amateur, college and professional association hires its own staff of minor officials.

You may also refer to Appendix E, which is a listing of private officiating schools and accredited college-level officiating courses throughout the United States. Initial contact should be made by telephone when making your inquiry concerning statistician, scorer and timekeeper courses.

Publications and periodicals are located in Appendix D. They will provide the serious individual with additional background and critical information on the sport.

The major manufacturers of sports-related equipment and supplies can be found in Appendix F. Each sport will require its officials to possess a proper uniform and other officiating equipment. These manufacturers can save you a tremendous amount of time and effort in locating exactly the right pieces of equipment.

COMPENSATION: At the amateur level, minor officials are compensated from $10 to $20 per game. At the college level, compensation ranges from $20 to $35, except for televised games, in which case, compensation is higher. At the professional level (AL, NL and NFL for example), officials are compensated $50 to $100 per game.

CHAPTER XXII

OTHER OFFICIATING OPPORTUNITIES

Since there are numerous opportunities available throughout the world within the sports officiating arena, this chapter will address those additional opportunities that should be seriously considered. Ostensibly, the same application procedure can be used to obtain certification.

For additional contacts and information on official rule books and application procedures pertaining to the various sports officiating opportunities listed in this chapter, contact your STATE HIGH SCHOOL ATHLETIC ASSOCIATION or THE NATIONAL FEDERATION OF STATE HIGH SCHOOL ATHLETIC ASSOCIATIONS for a copy of their current manuals. See Appendix A, which is a listing of all the high school athletic associations throughout the United States.

As previously instructed, the chapter on "Getting Started" will provide you with the step-by-step procedure needed to begin an officiating career.

Once you have become an official in one sport, you should consider becoming an official in another area. Most sports are seasonal. To maximize your income potential, you should qualify yourself in at least one or more of the following officiating areas listed below, thus avoiding periods when there is less demand for officiating in your primary area of interest.

Listed below in alphabetical order are national governing bodies. They will provide you with additional information pertaining to contacts, suggestions and procedures involved in becoming a sports official. Membership in one or more of these associations will be required.

The following sporting areas utilize numerous major and minor officials during their scheduled events. Compensation can range from $25 to $150 per event depending upon the level of experience plus travel and per diem.

NATIONAL ARCHERY ASSOCIATION (NAA), 1750 East Boulder Street, Colorado Springs, CO 80909 (303) 578-4576

U.S. BIATHLON ASSOCIATION, Adjutant General's Office, Camp Johnson, Bldg. 5, Winooski, VT 05404 (802) 655-0270, Ext. 22

U.S. BOBSLED & SKELETON ASSOCIATION, P.O. Box 828, Lake Placid, NY 12946 (518) 523-1842

AMERICAN CANOE ASSOCIATION (ACA), P.O. Box 248, Lorton, VA 22079 (703) 550-7523

U.S. CYCLING FEDERATION (USCF), 1750 East Boulder Street, Colorado Springs, CO 80909 (303) 578-4581

U.S.A. DIVING, INC. (USD), 901 West New York Street, Indianapolis, IN 46202 (317) 634-3040

AMERICAN HORSE SHOWS ASSOCIATION (AHSA), 598 Madison Avenue, New York, NY 10022

U.S. EQUESTRIAN TEAM (USET), 527 Madison Avenue, New York, NY 10022 (212) 753-1750

U.S. FENCING ASSOCIATION (USFA), 1750 East Boulder Street, Colorado Springs, CO 80909 (303) 578-4511

U.S. FIGURE SKATING ASSOCIATION (USFSA), 20 First Street, Colorado Springs, CO 80906 (303) 635-5200

UNITED STATES JUDO, INC. (USJ), P.O. Box 637, El Paso, TX 79944 (915) 541-7393

U.S. LUGE ASSOCIATION (USLA), Box 651, One Wilmington Rd., Lake Placid, NY 12946 (518) 523-2071

U.S. MODERN PENTATHLON ASSOCIATION, INC & U.S. MODERN PENTATHLON TRAINING CENTER, Ft. Sam Houston, TX 78234 (512) 221-4732

U.S. AMATEUR CONFEDERATION OF ROLLER SKATING, P.O. Box 83067, Lincoln, NE 68501 (402)483-7551

U.S. ROWING ASSOCIATION (USRA), #4 Boathouse Row, Philadelphia, PA 19130 (215) 769-2068

NATIONAL RIFLE ASSOCIATION (NRA), 1600 Rhode Island Avenue, NW, Washington, D.C. 20036 (202) 828-6255

U.S. SKI ASSOCIATION (USSA), 1750 East Boulder Street, Colorado Springs, CO 80909 (303) 578-4572

U.S. SKI TEAM (USST), P.O. Box 100, Park City, UT 84060 (801) 649-9090

U.S. INTERNATIONAL SPEEDSKATING ASSOCIATION (USISA), Beggs Isle, Oconomowoc, WI 53066 (414) 467-6051

U.S. SWIMMING, INC. (USS), 1750 East Boulder Street, Colorado Springs, CO 80909 (303) 578-4578

U.S. SYNCHRONIZED SWIMMING (USSS), 901 West New York Street, Indianapolis, IN 46202 (317) 633-2000

U.S. TABLE TENNIS ASSOCIATION (USTTA), 1750 East Boulder Street, Colorado Springs, CO 80909 (303) 578-4583

U.S. TEAM HANDBALL FEDERATION (USTHF), 1750 East Boulder Street, Colorado Springs, CO 80909 (303) 578-4582

UNITED STATES WATER POLO (USWP), 1750 East Boulder Street, Colorado Springs, CO 80909 (303) 578-4549

U.S. WEIGHTLIFTING FEDERATION (USWF), 1750 East Boulder Street, Colorado Springs, CO 80909 (303) 578-4508

U.S. YACHT RACING UNION (USYRU), P.O. Box 209, Newport, RI 02840 (401) 849-5200

NATIONAL WHEELCHAIR ATHLETIC ASSOCIATION, 2017 Templeton Gap Road, Suite C, Colorado Springs, CO 80907 (303) 632-0698

CONCLUSION

In the last ten years, there has been an enormous increase of interest in sports throughout the world. Baseball, football and basketball all began just over a hundred years ago and they are now considered major sports in many countries including the United States and Canada.

Most large cities, throughout the United states, have professional sports' teams and the cities reap the benefits of additional revenue. With the emergence of the USFL, more cities are seeking franchises. Newer and bigger enclosed stadiums are being built in anticipation of increased spectator participation for year round sporting events.

Sports and sports' coverage is now a multi-billion-dollar business. Every weekend of the year you can watch numerous sporting events on network television stations or cable.

The expansion of professional sports leagues has necessitated the employment of additional officials on the professional level. Employment opportunities have also increased on the amateur level and for beginning officials as schools, community centers, and colleges are expanding their sports programs and need qualified officials.

The opportunities are too numerous to mention and are available on a full-time or part-time basis. Now is the time to take advantage of them.

As illustrated throughout this book, the compensation in most instances is generous. Earnings will vary depending on the amount of time you invest and your level of achievement. The benefits are well worth the energy and time which you invest.

The legwork has been done, now you have the necessary formula for beginning your new career!!!

APPENDIX A

HIGH SCHOOL ATHLETIC ASSOCIATIONS

The names and addresses listed below should be contacted directly for applications, official high school rule books, case book material and certification requirements. Each of these associations are members of the National Federation. The number of high schools within each association is indicated in parentheses after the organization's name.

Alabama High School Athletic Assoc. (418 schools)
ATTN: Executive Director (205) 263-6994
926 Pelham Street, P.O. Box 5014, Montgomery, AL 36101

Alaska School Activities Association (149 schools)
ATTN: Executive Secretary (907) 563-3723
650 International Airport Rd., Anchorage, AK 99502

Arizona Interscholastic Assoc., Inc. (154 schools)
ATTN: Executive Director (602) 257-0272
2606 West Osborn Road, Phoenix, AZ 85017

Arkansas Activities Association (399 schools)
ATTN: Executive Director (501) 372-0383
1500 West 4th St., Little Rock, AR 72201

California Interscholastic Federation (1127 schools)
ATTN: Commissioner (714) 826-5390
2282 Rosecrans, Fullerton, CA 92633
(California is divided into ten sections. Candidates may have to call or write first to obtain the section of the state that would be most applicable).

Colorado High School Activities Assoc. (265 schools)
ATTN: Commissioner (303) 344-5050
11351 Montview Blvd., Aurora, CO 80010

Connecticut Interscholastic Athletic Conference (186)
ATTN: Executive Director (203) 281-1611
84 Linden Avenue, Hamden, CT 06518

Delaware Secondary School Athletic Assoc. (43)
ATTN: Executive Director (302) 736-4181
John G. Townsend Building, Dover, DE 19903

District of Columbia (17 schools)
ATTN: Supervising Director/Athletics (202) 724-4926
D.C. Public Schools, Lovejoy School,
12th & D Streets, N.E., Washington, DC 20002

Florida High School Activities Assoc. (464 schools)
ATTN: Executive Secretary (904) 372-9551
P.O. Box 1665, 240 First St., Gainesville, FL 32602

Georgia High School Association (367 schools)
ATTN: Executive Director (404) 647-7473
P.O. Box 271, 151 So. Bethel St., Thomaston, GA 30286

Hawaii High School Athletic Association (60 schools)
ATTN: Executive Secretary (808) 373-2720
941 Hind Luka Dr., Honolulu, HI 96821

Idaho High School Activities Assoc. (126 schools)
ATTN: Executive Director (208)244-1271
P.O. Box 2715, 2715 McGraw, Bloomington, IL 61701

Indiana High School Athletic Assoc. (401 schools)
ATTN: Commissioner (309) 663-6377
P.O. Box 40650, 9150 North Meridian Street
Indianapolis, IN 46240

Iowa High School Athletic Association (493 schools)
ATTN: Executive Secretary (515) 432-2011
P.O. Box 10, Boone, IO 50036

Kansas State High School Activities Assoc. (377)
ATTN: Executive Secretary (913) 235-9201
P.O. Box 495, 520 W. 27th St., Topeka, KA 66601

Kentucky High School Athletic Assoc. (299 schools)
ATTN: Commissioner (606) 252-4436
P.O. Box 22280, 560 E. Cooper, Lexington, KY 40522

Louisiana High School Athletic Assoc. (430 schools)
ATTN: Commissioner (504) 355-4680
P.O. Box 52778, Baton Rouge, LA 70892-2778

Maine Secondary School Principals Assoc. (141)
ATTN: Executive Director (207) 622-0217
15 Western Ave., Augusta, ME 04330

Maryland Public Secondary Schools Athletic Assoc. (153 schools)
ATTN: Executive Secretary (301) 659-2300
200 W. Baltimore St., Baltimore, MD 21201

Massachusetts Interscholastic Athletic Assoc. (357)
ATTN: Executive Director (617) 881-5750
P.O. Box 269, 75 Central St., Ashland, MA 01721

Michigan High School Athletic Assoc. (719 schools)
ATTN: Executive Director (517) 332-5046
1019 Trowbridge Road, East Lansing, MI 48823

Minnesota State High School League (502 schools)
ATTN: Executive Director (612) 427-5250
P.O. Box 309, 2621 Fairoak Ave., Anoka, MN 55303

Mississippi State High School Activities Assoc. (288)
ATTN: Director of Activities (601) 354-4117
P.O. Box 4521, 152 Millsaps Ave., Jackson, MS 39216

Missouri State High School Activities Assoc. (578)
ATTN: Executive Secretary (314) 445-4443
P.O. box 1328, 1808 I-70 Dr. SW, Columbia, MO 65205

Montana High School Association (190 schools)
ATTN: Executive Secretary (406) 442-6010
1 So. Dakota Ave., Helena, MT 59601

Nebraska School Activities Association (368 schools)
ATTN: Executive Director (402) 489-0386
P.O. Box 5463, 8230 Beechwood, Lincoln, NE 68505

Nevada Interscholastic Activities Association (59)
ATTN: Executive Director (702) 885-4390
400 W. King, Capital Complex, Carson City, NV 89710

New Hampshire Interscholastic Athletic Assoc. (87)
ATTN: Executive Director (603) 228-8671
P.O. Box 1215, 121 N. State St., Concord NH 03301

New Jersey State Interscholastic Athletic Assoc. (402)
ATTN: Executive Director (609) 587-4855
Route 130, P.O. Box 487, Robbinsville, NJ 08691

New Mexico Activities Association (126 schools)
ATTN: Executive Director (505) 2143-7991
P.O. Box 8407, 1721 University, Albuquerque, NM 87106

New York State Public High School Athletic Association (783 schools)
ATTN: Executive Director (518) 489-5471
P.O. Box 3567, Exec. Park So., Albany, NY 12203-3766

North Carolina High School Athletic Assoc. (334)
ATTN: Executive Director (919) 962-2345
P.O. Box 3216, UNC Campus, Chapel Hill, NC 27514

North Dakota High School Activities Assoc. (243)
ATTN: Executive Secretary (701) 845-3953
P.O. Box 817, 134 NE Third St., Valley City, ND 58072

Ohio High School Athletic Association (824 schools)
ATTN: Commissioner (614)267-2502
4080 Roselea Place, Columbus, OH 43214

Oklahoma Secondary School Activities Assoc. (490)
ATTN: Executive Secretary (405) 528-3385
Box 53464, 222 NE 27th St., Oklahoma City, OK 73152

Oregon School Activities Association (256 schools)
ATTN: Executive Director (503) 639-9656
1 Plaza SW, 6900 SW Haines Rd., Tigard, OR 97223

Pennsylvania Interscholastic Athletic Assoc. (660)
ATTN: Executive Director (717) 697-0374
Box 2008, 550 Gettysburg, Mechanicsburg, PA 17055

Rhode Island Interscholastic League, Inc. (59)
ATTN: Executive Director (401) 273-0530
Box 6367, 20 Regent Ave., Providence, RI 02908

South Carolina High School League (210 schools)
ATTN: Executive Director (803) 777-3116
RM 408, Carolina Coliseum, USC, Columbia, SC 29208

South Dakota High School Activities Association (208)
ATTN: Executive Secretary (605) 224-9261
Box 1217, 204 N. Euclid, Pierre, SD 57501

Tennessee Secondary School Athletic Assoc. (352)
ATTN: Executive Director (615) 889-6740
3333 Lebanon Rd., Hermitage, TN 37076

Texas University Interscholastic League (1154 schools)
ATTN: Director (512) 471-5883
P.O. Box 8028, 2622 Wichita St., Austin, TX 78712

Utah High School Activities Association (102 schools)
ATTN: Executive Director (801) 566-0681
199 East 7200 South, Midvale, UT 84047

Vermont Headmasters' Association, Inc. (77 schools)
ATTN: Executive Secretary (802) 229-0547
Box 128, 148 State St., Montpelier, VT 05602

Virginia High School League (286 schools)
ATTN: Executive Secretary (804) 924-7121
P.O. Box 3697, University Station,
Zehmer Building, 104 Midmont Lane, Charlottesville, VA 22903

Washington Interscholastic Activities Assoc. (347)
ATTN: Executive Director (206) 746-7102
4211 W. Lake Sammamish Blvd., Bellevue, WA 98998

West Virginia Secondary School Activities Commission
ATTN: Executive Secretary (304) 485-5494
Rt. 9, Box 76, Parkersburg, WV 26101

Wisconsin Interscholastic Athletic Assoc. (424)
ATTN: Executive Director (715) 344-8580
Box 267, 41 Park Ridge Dr., Stevens Point, WI 54481

Wyoming High School Activities Assoc. (72 schools)
ATTN: Executive Secretary (303) 577-0614
218 West 9th St., Casper, WY 82601

APPENDIX B

COLLEGIATE ATHLETIC CONFERENCES & ASSOCIATIONS

The following college conferences and associations should be contacted by experienced sports officials who have acquired at least a minimum of two years practical experience. These organizations can provide a sports official candidate with a broad range of information — especially information on the requirements for positions. Almost without exception, you should direct your telephone or mailing inquiries to the attention of the Information Director.

Atlantic Coast Conference, 2100 NW Cornwallace Drive, Greensborough, NC 47408 (919) 288-0208

Big Eight Conference, 600 East Eighth St., Kansas City, MO 64106 (816) 471-5088

Big Sky Conference, Box 1736, 409 West Jefferson, Boise, ID 83701 (208) 345-5393

Big Ten Conference, 1111 Plaza Drive, Schaumburg, IL 60195 (312) 438-4386

California Association of Community Colleges, 2017 "O" Street, Sacramento, CA 95814 (415) 345-4114

California Collegiate Athletic Association, 40 Via di Roma Walk, Long Beach, CA 90803 (714) 532-5561

Carolinas Intercollegiate Athletic Conference, High Point College, High Point, NC 27260 (919) 521-4214 249

Central Collegiate Conference, Western Michigan University, Kalamazoo, MI 49008 (618) 453-5311

Central Collegiate Hockey Association, 2000 West Henderson Rd., Columbus, OH 43220 (614) 457-3183

Central Intercollegiate Athletic Association, 2013 Cunningham Dr., Hampton, Va 23666 (804) 838-8801

Central States Intercollegiate Conference, 415 Kingsley, Liberty, MO 64068 (816) 271-4257

College Athletic Business Managers Association, Box 27, West Point, NY 10996 (817) 756-5487

College Athletic Conference, c/o University of The South, Sewanne, TN 37375 (615) 598-5931

College Conference of Illinois & Wisconsin, c/o North Park College, Chicago, IL 60625 (312) 583-2700

College Division Commissioner's Association, 2013 Cunningham Dr., Hampton, Va 23666 (804) 838-8801

College Football Association, Box 4148, Boulder, CO 80306(303) 449-1297

College Hockey Statistics Bureau, c/o University of Maine, Ofono, ME 04469 (207) 581-7376

College Swimming Coaches Association of America, 111 A Cooke Hall, University of Minnesota, Minneapolis, MN 55455 (612) 373-7547

Dixie Intercollegiate Athletic Conference, c/o North Carolina Wesleyan College, Rocky Mount, NC 27801 (919) 442-7121

Eastern College Athletic Conference, Box 3, Centerville, MA 02632 (617) 771-5060

Eastern Wrestling League, c/o Lock Haven State College, Lock Haven, PA 17745 (412) 624-4572

Evergreen Athletic Conference, (No address available) Information Director's Office (505) 838-1220 Ex 225

Far Western Conference, c/o San Francisco State University, San Francisco, CA 94132 (415) 469-1579

Florida Community College Activities Assn., 310 Collins Bldg., Tallahassee, FL 32301 (305) 685-4587

Garden State Athletic Conference, (No address available) (609) 586-4800

Golden Gate Conference, 321 Golf Club Road, Pleasant Hill, CA 94523 (415) 345-4114

Golf Coaches Assoc. of America, 1144 Lyn Rd., Bowling Green, OH 43402 (614)369-4431 Ex 500

Great Lakes Intercollegiate Athletic Conference, 414 Winter, Big Rapids, MI 49307 (616) 796-3804

Great Lakes Valley Conference, 2828 Danpatch, Lexington, KY 40511 (606) 252-4436

Gulf South Conference, 4 Office Park Circle-217, Birmingham, AL 35223 (205) 870-9750

Heartland Collegiate Conference, 2905 West Torquay Rd., Muncie, IN 47304 (317)285-4839

Hoosier Buckeye Collegiate Conference, 812 West Leggett, Wauseon, OH 43567 (419) 335-3686

Independent College Athletic Conference, c/o Ithaca College, Ithaca, NY 14850 (604) 274-3209

Intercollegiate Soccer Association of America, c/o Marist College, Poughkeepsie, NY 12601 (914) 471-3240

International Association of Approved Basketball Officials, Inc., Box 661, West Hartford, CT 06107 (203) 232-7530

Interregional Athletic Conference, c/o Jarvis Christian College, Hawkins, TX 75765 (214) 769-2174

Iowa Intercollegiate Athletic Conference, 1615 West Shrock Rd., Waterloo, IA 50701 (319) 296-2227

IVY Group, 70 Washington Rd., Princeton, NJ 08540 (609) 452-6426

JC Athletic Bureau, Box 5401, San Mateo, CA 94402 (415) 345-4114

Kansas College Athletic Conference, 6940 Newell, Wichita, KS 67212 (316) 947-3121 Ext. 213

Keystone Athletic Conference, c/o Penn State Capitol Campus, Middletown, PA 17057 (717) 948-6267

Lone Star Conference, 500 Franklin Dr., San Marcos, TX 78666 (512) 595-3203

Madison Square Garden, 4 Pennsylvania Plaza, New York NY 10001 (215) 563-8100

Metro Conference, 7777 Bonhomme Ave., 1501, St. Louis, MO 63105 (314) 862-6011

Metropolitan Intercollegiate Football Conference, c/o St. Johns University, Jamaica, NY 11439 (212) 990-6224

Michigan Community College Athletic Association,143 Bostwick, Grand Rapids, MI 49503 (616) 456-4864

Michigan Intercollegiate Athletic Association, Box 63, Spring Lake, MI 49456 (616) 842-7865

Mid-American Conference, 2000 West Henderson Road, #230, Columbus, OH 43220 (614) 457-3183

Mid-Continent Conference, 2127 South Oneida, Green Bay, WI 54304 (414) 494-4494

Mid-Eastern Athletic Conference, Box 21205, Greensboro, NC 27420 (919) 275-9961

Midwestern City Conference, 509 Park Lane Dr., Champaing, IL 61820 (314) 862-1324

Minnesota Community College Conference, 550 Cedar, St. Paul, MN 55010 (612) 296-3758

Minnesota Intercollegiate Athletic Conference, 405 Laurie Ln., Stillwater, MN 55082 (612) 439-7768

Missouri Valley Conference, 6111 East Skelly Dr. 702, Tulsa, OK 74135 (918) 664-9245

National Association of Collegiate Directors of Athletics, 1229 Smith Court, Rocky River, OH 44116 (216) 331-5773

National Association of Intercollegiate Athletics (NAIA) 1221 Baltimore, Kansas City, Missouri (816) 842-5050

National Christian College Athletic Association, 1815 Union Avenue, Chattanooga, TN 37404 (615) 698-6021

National Collegiate Athletic Association (NCAA), Box 1906, Mission, KS 66201 (913) 384-3220

National Collegiate Football Association, 15 Tulipwood Dr., Commack, NY 11725 (516) 543-0730

NCAA Division I Track Coaches Association, 1706 Evanston, Kalamazoo, MI 49008 (616) 383-1338

National Intercollegiate Squash Racquets Association c/o Dartmount College, Hanover, NH 03755 (914) 938-4689

National Jr. College Athletic Association, Box 1586, Hutchinson, KS 67501 (316) 663-5445

National Soccer Coaches Association of America, Rd #5 Box 5074, Stroudsburg, PA 18360 (717) 421-8720

National Wrestling Coaches Association, Box 8002, Salt Lake City, UT (801) 581-3836

Nebraska College Conference, c/o Kearney State College, Kearney, NE 68847 (308) 236-4192

New England Collegiate Conference, Southern Connecticut State College, New Haven, CT 06515 (203) 576-4734

New England University Wrestling Association, c/o University of New Hampshire, Durham, NH 03824 (603) 862-1850

New Jersey Sports & Exposition Authority, East Rutherford, NJ 07073 (201) 460-4367

New Jersey State College Athletic Conference, c/o Montclair State College, Upper Montclair, NJ 07043 (201) 893-5234

New York Athletic Conference (SUNY), c/o Fredonia State, Fredonia, NY 14063 (716) 673-3102

North Central Intercollegiate Athletic Conference, 2400 N. Louise, Sioux Fall, SD 47107 (605) 338-0907

Northeast-8 conference, c/o Bentley College, Waltham, MA 02254 (617)891-2256

Northeastern Athletic Conference, c/o College of St. Rose, Albany, NY 12203 (518) 482-2435

Northeast California Baseball Association, 51 Oak Knoll Loop, Walnut Creek, CA 94596 (415) 939-6235

Northern Illinois Intercollegiate Conference, Box 159, Kankakee, IL 60901 (815) 939-5372

Ohio Athletic Conference, 2000 W. Henderson Rd., #230, Columbus, OH 43220 (614) 457-6837

Ohio Valley Conference, 4205 Hillsboro Rd., #304-B, Nashville, TN 37215 (615) 327-2557

Old Dominion Athletic Conference, Box 971, Calem, VA 24153 (703) 463-9111

Pacific Coast Athletic Association, 1700 East Dyer Rd., 140, Santa Ana, CA 92705 (714) 979-0353

Pacific Soccer Conference, c/o University of Calif., Berkeley, CA 94720 (415) 497-1021

Pacific-10 Conference, 800 S. Broadway, 400, Walnut Creek, CA 94596 (415) 932-4411

Rocky Mountain Athletic Conference, 2940 East Bates, Denver, CO 80210 (303) 433-8645

Southeastern Athletic Conference, 1658 Kings Road, Jacksonville, FL 32209 (803) 534-2710

Southeastern Conference, 1214 Central Bank Building, Birmingham, AL 35233 (205) 252-7415

Southern California Baseball Association, 1700 East Dyer Rd., 140, Santa Ana, CA 92705 (714) 979-0353

Southern California Conference, 812 Sixth Street, Manhatten Beach, CA 90266 (714) 826-2220

Southern Christian Athletic Conference, c/o Bryan College, Dayton, TN 37321 (615) 775-2041

Southern Conference, 55 Woodlawn Green 220, Charlotte, NC 28210 (704) 527-0314

Southern Intercollegiate Athletic Conference, Box 311, Normal, AL 35762 (205) 825-6209

Southland Conference, Box 1627, Shreveport, LA 71165 (318) 747-9023

Southwest Athletic Conference, Box 47420, Dallas, TX 75247 (214) 634-7353

Southwestern Athletic Conference, Box 689, Lorman MS 39096 (601) 254-6641

Sun Belt Conference, 1408 N. Westshore Blvd., 1010 Tampa, FL 33607 (813) 872-1511

Sunshine State Conference, Box 906, Maitland, FL 32751 (305) 625-6000 Ext. 160

Texas Eastern Conference, 1205 Columbia Circle, Corsicana, TX 75110 (214) 872-3931

Texas Intercollegiate Athletic Association, 900 N. Grand, Sherman, TX 75090 (817) 968-9074

Texas Junior College Athletic Conference, 911 Boling Highway, Wharton, TX 77488 (713) 532-4560

Trans America Athletic Conference, 7505 Pines 1255, Shreveport, LA 71129 (318) 686-7111

Tri-State College Bowling Conference, 1215 Wilbraham, Springfield, MA 01119 (413)782-3111 Ex 220

U. S. Baseball Federation, 4 Gregory Drive, Hamilton Square, NJ 08690 (609) 586-2381

U. S. Olympic Committee, 1750 E. Boulder St., Colorado Springs, CO 80909 (303) 578-4531

U. S. Soccer Federation, 350 Fifth Avenue No. 4010, New York, NY 10018 (212) 736-0915

West Coast Athletic Conference, 51 Oak Knoll Loop, Walnut Creek, CA 94596 (415) 355-7000 Ext. 258

West Virginia Intercollegiate Athletic Conference, 1029 Quincy St., Parkersburg, WV 26101 (304) 485-3958

Western Athletic Conference, 1515 Cleveland Place 300, Denver, CO 80202 (303) 534-0217

Western States Conference, 812 Sixth St., Manhatten Beach, CA 90266 (805) 642-3211

Wisconsin Collegiate Conference, Box 8010, Madison, WI 53708 (608) 263-4402

Wisconsin State University Conference, Box 8010, Madison, WI 53708 (608) 263-4402

Women's Basketball Poll, 6613 Akron St., Philadelphia, PA (800) 523-4510

Yankee Conference, c/o University of New Hampshire, Durham, NH 03824 (603) 862-1850

MISC.

Association for Intercollegiate Athletics for Women, 1201 16th St., NW, Washington, DC 20036

College Athletic Business Managers Association, University of Iowa, Iowa City, IA 52242

APPENDIX C

PROFESSIONAL ORGANIZATIONS & ASSOCIATIONS

Additional information on specific qualifications for employment as an official is available from the following professional organizations.

They are able to provide information reference their own organizational structure and criteria.

If you are ready to advance to the professional level, contact the appropriate organization(s) listed below:

BASKETBALL:

National Basketball Association (NBA), 645 Fifth Avenue, New York, NY 10022 (212)826-7000

FOOTBALL:

American Football Coaches Association, Box 8705 Durham, NC 27707

National Football League (NFL), 410 Park Avenue, New York, NY 10022 (212) 758-1500

United States Football League (USFL), 52 Vanderbilt, 4th Fl., New York, NY 10017 (212) 682-6363

BASEBALL:

American League Baseball, 280 Park Avenue, New York, NY 10017 (212) 371-7600

Association of Professional Ball Players of America, 337 E. San Antonio Drive, 203, Long Beach, CA 90807 (213) 423-5258

International League of Professional Baseball Clubs, P.O. Box 608, Grove City, OH 43123 (614) 871-1300

National Association of Leagues, Umpires & Scorers, Box 1420, Wichita, KS 67201

National Association of Professional Baseball Leagues, P.O. Box A, 225 Fourth Street So., St. Petersburg, FL 33731

National Association of Professional Baseball Minor Leagues, St. Petersburg, FL (813) 822-6937

National Baseball Congress, Box 1420, Wichita, KS 67201

National League of Professional Baseball Clubs, One, Rockefeller Plaza, New York, NY 10020 (212) 371-7300

FOOTBALL (CANADA):

Canadian Football League (CFL), 11 Kings Street West, Suite 1800, Toronto, Ontario M4H1A3 (416) 366-8591

Canadian Football League Officiating Supervisory Staff, 37 Kings Knowe Road, Rexdale, Ontario M9W 4C1 (416) 366-8591

Eastern Football Conference (EFC), Box 172, Hamilton, Ontario L8N 3A2 (416) 527-1508

Western Football Conference (WFC), 1221 Jubilee Ave., Regina, Saskatchewan S4S 3S7 (306)586-2505

SOCCER:

National Soccer Coaches Association of America, 668 La Vista Road, Walnut Creek, CA 94598

North America Soccer League (NASL), 113 Avenue of the Americas, New York, NY 10036

Major Indoor Soccer League (MISL), 1 Bala Cynwyd Plaza, Suite 415, Bala Cynwyd, PA 19004 (215) 667-8020

TENNIS:

National Indoor Tennis Association (NITA), P.O. Box 11097, Chicago, IL 60611 (312) 943-5933

United States Professional Tennis Association, 6701 Highway 58, Harrison, TN 37341 (615) 344-8397

United States Tennis Association, 51 East 42nd Street, New York, NY 10017 (212) 949-9112

GOLF:

Professional Golfers Association of America (PGA), Box 12458, Lake Park, FL 33403

HOCKEY:

American Hockey League, 31 Elm Street, Suite 533, Springfield, MA 01103 (413) 781-2030

National Hockey League, 920 Sun Life Building, Montreal, PQ, Canada H3B 2W2 (514) 871-9220

BOXING:

International Veteran Boxers Association, 94 Crescent Ave., New Rochelle, NY 10801

United States Boxing Federation, 1750 E. Boulder St., Boulder, CO 80909 (513) 281-4400

World Boxing Association, 412 Colorado Avenue, Aurora, IL 60506 (312) 897-4765

World Boxing Council, North American Boxing Federation, P.O. Box 12157, Capitol Station, Austin, TX 78711 (512) 475-4229

ARCHERY:

National Archery Association of the United States, 1951 Geraldson Dr., Lancaster, PA 17601

VOLLEYBALL:

United States Volleyball Association, 557 Fourth Street, San Francisco, CA 94107

TRACK & FIELD:

United States Track & Field Federation, 30 Norton Avenue, Tucson, AZ 85719

BOWLING:

American Bowling Congress, 5301 South 76th St., Greendale, WI 53129

American Junior Bowling Congress, 5301 South 76th St., Greendale, WI 53129

Professional Bowlers Association of America, 1720 Merriman Road, Akron, OH 44313

Professional Women Bowlers Association, 205 West Wacker Dr., Suite 300, Chicago, IL 60606

HORSE RACING:

Thoroughbred Club of America, P.O. Box 8147, Lexington, KY 40503
United States Trotting Association, 750 Michigan Avenue, Columbus, OH 43215

AMATEUR ORGANIZATIONS:

Amateur Athletic Union of the United States, 3400 W. 86th St., Indianapolis, IN 46268
Amateur Hockey Association of the United States, 10 Lake Circle, Colorado Springs, CO 80906
Golden Gloves Association of America, 8801 Princess Jeanne NE, Alberquerque, NM 87112 (505)298-9286
International Joint Rules Committee of Softball, 2731 NE 14th St. # 524-B, Causeway, FL
International Softball Federation, 2801 NE 50th St., Oklahoma City, OK 73111 (405) 424-5266
Little League Baseball, Williamsport, PA 17701
Pop Warner Junior League Football, 1315 Walnut Street, Suite 606, Philadelphia, PA 19107
United States Amateur Jai Alai Players Association, 100 SE Second Avenue, Miami, FL 33131

OLYMPICS:

International Olympics Committee, Chateau de Vidy, Ch-1007, Lausanne, Switzerland
United States Olympic Committee, 57 Park Avenue, New York, NY 10016
Amateur Athletic Union (AAU/USA), Junior Olympics, 3400 West 86th Street, P.O. Box 68207, Indianapolis, IN 46268 (317) 872-2900

APPENDIX D

PUBLICATIONS & MAGAZINES

To keep abreast of the profession, especially in terms of changes, new decisions and rulings, it is recommended that an aspiring official subscribe to one or more of the following publications or magazines. Available literature will help provide additional knowledge and understanding of a particular sport or group of sports. If the publication is not readily available in your area newsstand, you can ask your local library to locate and order the publication or write directly to the address(es) listed below:

ATHLETIC JOURNAL, 1719 Howard Street, Evanston, IL 60202

BASEBALL DIGEST, 1020 Church Street, Evanston, IL 60201

THE BASKETBALL CLINIC, Parker Publishing Co., West Nyack, NY 10994

BASKETBALL DIGEST, 1020 Church Street, Evanston, IL 60201

BASKETBALL NEWS, 114 Madison Avenue, Coral Gables, FL 33134

BASKETBALL WEEKLY, 19830 Mack Avenue, Grosse Pointe, MI 48236

BLACK SPORTS, 31 East 28th Street, New York, NY 10016

BOWLING DIGEST, 1020 Church Street, Evanston, IL 60201

COACH AND ATHLETE, 200 S. Hull Street, Montgomery, AL 36104

FIELD & STREAM, 1515 Broadway, New York, NY 10036

FOOTBALL DIGEST, 1020 Church Street, Evanston, IL 60201

FOOTBALL NEWS, 19830 Mack Avenue, Grosse Pointe, MI 48236

GOLF DIGEST, 495 Westport Avenue, Norwalk, CT 06856

HOCKEY DIGEST, 1020 Church Street, Evanston, IL 60201

INSIDE SPORTS, 1020 Church Street, Evanston, IL 60201

MUSCLE & FITNESS, 2100 Erwin Street, Woodland Hills, CA 91317

NATIONAL COACH, 3423 East Silver Springs Boulevard, Ocala, FL 32670

OUTDOOR LIFE, 380 Madison Avenue, New York, NY 10017

PGA MAGAZINE, 100 Avenue of the Champions, P.O. Box 12458, Palm Beach Garden, FL 33410

REFEREE, P.O. Box 161, Franksville, WI 53126 (Note: This publication is considered by many to be one of the best publications available on the market).

THE RING/BOXING ILLUSTRATED, 120 West 31st Street, New York, NY 10001

THE RUNNER'S WORLD, 1400 Stierlin Road, P.O. Box 366, Mountain View, CA 94043

SCHOLASTIC COACH, Scholastic Coach, Inc., 50 West 44th Street, New York, NY 10036

SOCCER DIGEST, 1020 Church Street, Evanston, IL 60201

SPORTS AFIELD MAGAZINE, 250 West 55 Street, New York, NY 10019

SPORTS ILLUSTRATED, 541 North Fairbanks Ct., Chicago, IL 60611

SKIN DIVER, Peterson Publishing Co., 5959 Hollywood Boulevard, Los Angeles, CA 90028

SPORT, McFadden-Bartell Corp., 205 East 42nd Street, New York, NY 10017

SPORTING NEWS, 1212 North Lindbegh, St. Louis, MO 63166

SPORTS WOMAN, 119 Paul Drive, Rafael, CA 94903

SWIMMING WORLD, 8622 Bellanca, Los Angeles, CA 90045

TENNIS, 495 Westport Avenue, P.O. Box 5350, Norwalk, CT 06856

TRACK AND FIELD NEWS, P.O. Box 296, Los Altos, CA 94022

WOMENSPORTS, Women's Sport Publishing Co., 1660 South Amphlet Boulevard, San Mateo, CA 50306

WORLD TENNIS, 383 Madison Avenue, New York, NY 10017

APPENDIX E

OFFICIATING SCHOOLS

Throughout the United States you will discover that many universities, junior colleges, recreation departments and high schools offer accredited courses and studies on being an official. For example, Ohio University offers a full range of officiating courses.

Major universities can supply an aspiring official with in-depth instruction in the art of officiating. In addition, you may want to seriously consider a private officiating school that offers specialized study on a specific sport activity. The purpose of these schools is to provide supervised training for prospective umpires and other sports officials so that the individual can qualify for positions in professional, semi-professional, college, high school and amateur sports.

Private training camps usually cost more to attend; however, they tend to take a very practical approach to officiating as those in attendance are all preparing themselves specifically for certification. The cost for attending ranges from $100 to $400 for a three to six day clinic and from $500 to 1500 for a four to five wek course. You should check to make sure that the cost covers food and lodging-in many cases this is extra. In order to expedite a career at the college and professional levels, these camps and officiating schools are a MUST!

PRIVATE SCHOOLS

BASEBALL:

Joe Brinkman Umpires School — (813) 825-0953
1223 13th Street North
St. Petersburg, FL 33705

Joe Brinkman Umpires School — (714) 887-6444
San Bernardino, CA 92407

Barnie Deary (Minor League Development Program)
St. Petersburg, FL 33705

Bill Kinnamon Umpires School (813) 393-9711
9700 Starkey Road, #214
Largo, FL 33543

Bill Kinnamon Umpires School (714) 887-6444
c/o Little League Baseball
6707 Little League Drive
San Bernardino, CA 92407

Harry Wendelstedt School For Umpires
88 South Street
Andrews Dr., Ormond Beach, FL 32074

BASKETBALL:

All American Basketball Officials Clinic
c/o Bill Herzog
405 Laurie Lane
Stillwater, MN 55082

Atlanta ProAm Camp
c/o Derek Stafford (404) 761-6953
Blue Chip Officials Camp
c/o Ed Trexler, Director
2076 Minton Dr., Tempe, AZ 85282

Chicago Midwest Basketball Camp
c/o Rubin Norris, Coordinator (312) 294-2354
St. Anselem's R. C. Gym, 210 East 61st Street, Chicago, IL 60637

European Try-Out Camp (East Coast)
c/o Richard Kaner (201) 333-2059
2541 Jf Kennedy Boulevard
St. Peter's College, Jersey City, NJ 07306

European Try-Out Camp (Southeastern)
c/o Al Kyber, Coach (803) 329-2140
Winthrop College, Rock Hill, SC 29730

European Try-Out Camp (West Coast)
c/o Steve Patterson (707) 527-4374
Santa Rosa Junior College, Santa Rosa, CA

Irv Brown Basketball Officiating Camp
Irv Brown Camp (714) 279-7800
8245 Ronson Road
San Diego, CA 92111

Jack Manton Basketball Referee Camp
112 West Main St., Cumming, CA 30130

Kawaga Sports Camp
c/o Ron Silverstein
2235 Grandview Place
Glenview, IL 60025

Midwest Umpiring Training School
3612 South 55th Avenue (312) 652-5567
Cicero, IL 60650

National Pro Referee School (212) 725-1800
c/o Dick Bavetta
Suite 1700, 475 Park Avenue So., New York, NY 10016

NBA Camps and NBA/ProAm Camps
c/o Cecil K. Watkins (212) 826-7000
National Basketball Association, Olympic Tower — 645 Fifth Avenue, New York, NY 10022

New York Metro ProAm Officials Association (Camp)
c/o Sylvester Dobson, Coordinator (201) 733-6790

Southeast Basketball Referee Camp
c/o Charlie Vacca (615) 749-3521
704 Stone Creek Ct.
Nashville, TN 37221

Superstar Basketball Officiating Camp
c/o Bob Herrold (800) 542-6005
8245 Ronson Road, Suite D 601
San Diego, CA 92111

Annual Pro Basketball Referees Camp
c/o Hue S. Hollins (714) 629-6803
7 Pepperwood Circle, Pomona, CA 91766

FOOTBALL:

Blue Chip Officials Camp
c/o Ed Trexler, Director
2076 Minton Dr., Temple, AZ 85282

West Coast Football Officials Clinic
c/o Dr. Laird Hayes, Director (714) 642-6336
1630 Mariners Drive
Newsport Beach, CA 92660

HOCKEY:

International School of Refereeing (NHL Officials)
Refereeing
383 Highside Drive
Milton, Ontario, Canada L9T 1W9

PARTIAL LIST OF ACCREDITED COLLEGE OFFICIATING COURSES

UNIVERSITY OF ALABAMA, P.O. Box 1408, Rose Administration Building, University, AL 35486 (205)348-7200

Techniques of officiating major sports, rules interpretation and lab experience. Teaching and officiating gymnastics.

UNIVERSITY OF ALASKA-FAIRBANKS, Fairbanks, AK 99701

Judging and coaching gymnastics, administrating men's and women's gymnastics.

UNIVERSITY OF ALBUQUERQUE, St. Joseph Place, NW, Albuquerque, NM 87140

Theory and practice of officiating.

ALLEGHENY COLLEGE, Meadville, PA 16335

Officiating courses offered in intramural, intercollegiate and community sports.

ALMA COLLEGE, Alma, MI 48801 1/800-248-9267

Officiating courses offered in strategy, rules and responsibilities of football, coaching baseball, track and field, basketball, field hockey, volleyball.

ANDERSON COLLEGE, Anderson, IN 46011

Emphasis is on coaching.

AQUINAS COLLEGE, Grand Rapids, MI 49506 (800) 545-0055

Officiating courses offered in basketball, baseball, softball, volleyball. Michigan certification program available.

ASBURY COLLEGE, Wilmore, KY 40390 (606) 858-3511

General officiating course offered.

UNIVERSITY OF ARIZONA, Tucson, AZ 85721 (602) 626-3237

Officiating courses offered in basketball, baseball, softball, women's gymnastics, football, wrestling, field hockey and soccer.

ASHLAND COLLEGE, Founders Hall, Ashland, OH 44805 (419) 289-4142

Officiating courses offered in baseball, basketball, field hockey, football, softball, track, volleyball and wrestling. Certification in High School Athletics available.

AUBURN UNIVERSITY, Auburn, AL 36830

Officiating courses offered in football, basketball, softball and volleyball.

AUGSBURG COLLEGE, 731 21st Avenue South, Minneapolis, MN 55454 (612) 300-1001

Primarily offers coaching courses.

BALDWIN-WALLACE COLLEGE, 275 Eastland Road, Berea, OH 44017 (216) 826-2222

Officiating courses offered in acquisition theory and techniques necessary for becoming a rated official. Other officiating courses offered include: basketball, football, soccer, track & field, volleyball and wrestling.

BENEDICTINE COLLEGE, Atchison, KS 66002 (913) 367-5340

Officiating courses emphasis team sports such as baseball, basketball, football and volleyball.

BEREA COLLEGE, Berea, KY 40404

Officiating courses include women's basketball and volleyball stressing nationwide standards.

BERRY COLLEGE, Mount Berry, GA 30149

Studies include officiating team sports such as basketball, volleyball, football and soccer.

BLOOMSBURG STATE COLLEGE, Pennsylvania 17815

Officiating studies include basketball, baseball, football, cross country, track and field, field hockey, wrestling and swimming.

BOB JONES UNIVERSITY, Greenville SC 29614 (803) 242-5100

Courses offered in officiating major and minor sports.

BOISE STATE UNIVERSITY, 1910 University Drive, Boise, ID 83725 (208) 385-1011

Officiating studies include intramurals and sports designed to acquaint students with organization and administration of intramural programs and officiating same.

BRADLEY UNIVERSITY, Peoria, IL 61625 (800) 447-6460

Sports officiating studies include techniques of various team and individual sports, lab experience included.

BRIAR CLIFF COLLEGE, 3303 Redecca St., Sioux City, IA 51104 (712) 279-5321

Offers techniques of officiating team sports designed to acquaint students with fundamental sports programming, implementation and supervision. Related areas include management of officiating events such as track, swimming, wrestling, gymnastics.

BUTLER UNIVERSITY, 46th at Sunset Avenue, Indianapolis, IN 46208

Offers procedures for officiating football, basketball and baseball.

CALIFORNIA STATE COLLEGE STANISLAUS, Turlock, CA 95380 (209) 667-3122

Studies include interpretation of rules for various sports, procedures, mechanics and practice officiating in such sports as: football, basketball, baseball, track and field.

CALIFORNIA STATE UNIVERSITY, Dominquez Hills, Carsan, CA 90747 (213) 516-3300

Studies include baseball, softball, volleyball and track.

CALIFORNIA STATE UNIVERSITY, Fullerton, 400 Golden Gate, Long Beach, CA 92634 (213) 590-5506

Studies include techniques of officiating sports, rules necessary for officiating team sports.

CALIFORNIA STATE UNIVERSITY, Hayward, CA 94542 (415) 881-3000
Officiating sports includes theory and practical experience in officiating men's and women's sports.

CALIFORNIA STATE UNIVERSITY, Los Angeles, 5151 State University Dr., Los Angeles, CA 90032
Studies include basketball, football, volleyball and softball.

CASE WESTERN RESERVE UNIVERSITY, 2040 Adelbert Road, Cleveland, OH 44106
Officiating sports (general).

CEDARVILLE COLLEGE, Box 601, Cedarville, OH 45314 (513) 766-2211
Officiating studies include basketball and volleyball.

CENTRAL CONNECTICUT STATE COLLEGE, New Britain, CT 06050 827-7543

CENTRAL STATE UNIVERSITY, Wilberforce, OH 45384 (513) 376-6478
Football, basketball, and volleyball.

CLARENDON COLLEGE, P.O. Box 968, Clarendon, TX 79226 (806) 874-3571
Major sports.

COCHISE COLLEGE, Douglas, AZ 85607 (602) 364-7943
Basketball, football, baseball and volleyball.

THE COLLEGE OF MOUNT ST. JOSEPH ON THE OHIO, Mount St. Joseph, OH 45051
Theory and practice of officiating sports.

COLLEGE OF THE REDWOODS, Eureka, CA 95501 (707) 443-8411
Volleyball, women's basketball, softball, men's football, men's basketball, men's track, men's baseball. Studies include advance officiating courses.

CONCORDIA COLLEGE, 7400 Augusta Street, River Forest, IL 60305 (312) 771-8300
Studies include fall, winter and spring sports.

CONCORDIA COLLEGE, Hamline & Marshall, St. Paul, MN 55104

Football, basketball, soccer, softball, track & field, volleyball and wrestling.

CONCORDIA COLLEGE, Moorhead, MN 56560

Coaching & officiating competitive sports such as baseball, football, basketball, gymnastics, hockey, track and field, volleyball and wrestling.

CREIGHTON UNIVERSITY, P.O. Box 3266, Omaha, NE 68131 (402) 280-2700

Sports officiating (general).

CULVER-STOCKTAN COLLEGE, College-Hall, Cantan, MO 63435

Officiating sports courses include football, swimming, wrestling, baseball, track & field.

CYPRESS COLLEGE, 9200 Valley View Street, Cypress, CA 90630 (714) 826-2220

Officiating courses include men's sports (football, water polo, cross country, wrestling and soccer). Womens officiating courses include: aquatics, basketball, volleyball, hockey and softball.

DAKOTA WESLEYAN UNIVERSITY, Mitchell, SD 57301 (605) 996-6511

Officiating courses offered in football and basketball, wrestling, and softball.

DENISON UNIVERSITY, Box H, Granville, OH 43023

Officiating course offered in football and basketball.

UNIVERSITY OF DETROIT, 4001 West McMichaels, Detroit, MI 48221 (313) 927-1000

Rules and officiating courses offered in football, basketball, track & field. Women's officiating courses offered in field hockey, volleyball and softball.

DePAUW UNIVERSITY, Greencastle, IN 46135-0037

Officiating courses offered in field hockey, football, basketball, track & field, baseball, softball, soccer, volleyball and wrestling.

UNIVERSITY OF DENVER, Denver, CO 80208 (303) 753-2036

General officiating course offered.

DICKINSON COLLEGE, Carlisle, PA 17013
Officiating course in volleyball.

DICKINSON STATE COLLEGE, Dickinson, ND 58601
Officiating courses offered in gymnastics, plus women's officiating courses in basketball, softball and volleyball, and men's officiating courses in basketball, baseball and football.

EAST CAROLINE UNIVERSITY, Greenville, NC 27834
Officiating courses offered in football, touch and flag football, volleyball, basketball and softball.

EASTERN MICHIGAN UNIVERSITY, Ypsilanti, MI 48197
Officiating courses offered in officiating both men's and women's sports.

EASTERN MONTANA COLLEGE, Billings, MT 59102 (406) 657-2011
General sports officiating course.

EASTERN NEW MEXICO UNIVERSITY, Portales, N.M. 88130
General sports officiating course.

ELMHURST COLLEGE, Elmhurst, IL 60126 (312) 279-4100
Officiating courses offered in basketball, wrestling and baseball.

EMORY & HENRY COLLEGE, Emory, VA 24327 (703) 944-3121
Coaching and officiating courses in football, basketball, baseball, track & field.

EMPORIA STATE UNIVERSITY, 1200 Commercial, Emporia, KS 66801
Rules & mechanics of officiating men's and women's sports.

UNIVERSITY OF EVANSVILLE, P.O. Box 329, Evansville, IN 47702 (812) 479-2468
General officiating course.

FERRIS STATE COLLEGE, Big Rapids, MI 49307 (616) 796-0461
Officiating courses offered in basketball and football.

FLORIDA SOUTHERN COLLEGE, Lakeland, FL 33802
Officiating course offered in team sports.

FLORIDA STATE UNIVERSITY, Tallahassee, FL 32306
General officiating course.

FOOTHILL COLLEGE, 1234 El Mante Road, Los Altos Hills, CA 94022
Officiating courses offered in football, basketball, baseball, water polo, soccer, track & field.

FORT HAYS STATE UNIVERSITY, KS 67601 1-800-432-0248
Officiating course, general.

FULLERTON COLLEGE, 321 East Chapman Avenue, Fullerton, CA 92634 (714) 871-8000
Officiating courses offered in men's sports (football, basketball, baseball, softball, track & field), and women's sports (basketball, volleyball, badminton, tennis, softball and swimming).

GEORGE FOX COLLEGE, Newberg, OR 97131 (503) 538-8383 Ext: 234
Rules and officiating courses offered in football, basketball, volleyball and softball.

GEORGE MASON UNIVERSITY, 4400 University Drive, Fairfax, VA 22030
Course offered in officiating and intramural administration.

GLEN OAKS COMMUNITY COLLEGE, Centerville, MI 49032 (616) 467-9945
Officiating courses offered in football, basketball, track & field.

GLASSBORO STATE COLLEGE, Glassboro, NJ 08028 (604) 445-5000
Officiating course offered in competitive swimming and diving.

HARDIN-SIMMONS UNIVERSITY, Abilene, TX 79601 (915) 677-7281
Coaching and officiating courses offered in football, baseball, basketball, track & field, soccer and volleyball.

GRACE COLLEGE, Winona Lake, IN 46590
Course offered in methods of officiating.

HAMLINE UNIVERSITY, College of Liberal Arts, St. Paul, MN 55104

Officiating courses offered in football, basketball, track & field, baseball, softball, hockey, wrestling, gymnastics and volleyball.

HOUGHTON COLLEGE, Houghton, NY 14744

Officiating courses offered in football, field hockey, soccer, basketball, volleyball, swimming, track, baseball and softball.

MICHIGAN TECHNOLOGICAL UNIVERSITY, Houghtan, MI 49931

Officiating courses offered in basketball, volleyball, hockey and softball.

ILLINOIS WESLEYAN UNIVERSITY, Bloomington, IL 61701

General sports officiating course.

ILLINOIS STATE UNIVERSITY, Normal, IL 61761 (309) 438-2111

Officiating courses offered in basketball, badminton, field hockey, swimming, volleyball, track & field, softball, gymnastics and tennis.

UNIVERSITY OF IOWA, Iowa City, IA 52242

Officiating courses offered in football, basketball and baseball.

INDIANA STATE UNIVERSITY, Terre Haute, IN 47809

Officiating courses offered in basketball, football, boy's and girl's gymnastics, volleyball.

INDIANA UNIVERSITY OF PENNSYLVANIA, Indiana, PA 15705 (412) 357-2100

Officiating courses offered in volleyball and basketball.

IOWA WESLEYAN COLLEGE, Mt. Pleasant, IA 52641 (319) 385-8021

Officiating courses offered in major sports (general).

KENNESAW COLLEGE, Marietta, GA 30061 (404) 429-2700

Officiating courses offered in individual and team sports.

JOHNSON STATE COLLEGE, Johnson, VT 05656 (802) 635-2356

General officiating course.

LANGSTON UNIVERSITY, P.O. Box 728, Langston, OK 73050

Officiating courses offered in basketball, football, track and baseball.

LANE COMMUNITY COLLEGE, 4000 East 30th Avenue, Eugene, OR 97405

Officiating course in soccer.

KENTUCKY WESLEYAN COLLEGE, 3000 Frederria Street, Owensboro, KY 42301 (502) 926-3111

Course offered in techniques of officiating.

KENTUCKY STATE UNIVERSITY, Frankfort, KY 40601

Officiating courses offered in basketball, track, baseball, tennis and golf; plus women's officiating courses in field hockey, volleyball, basketball, softball and tennis.

LENOIR COMMUNITY COLLEGE, P.O. Box 188, Kinston, NC 28501 (919) 527-6223

Course offered in officiating (general).

LINDENWOOD COLLEGE, St. Charles, MO 63301 (314) 946-6912

Officiating techniques.

THE BROOKLYN UNIVERSITY OF NEW YORK, Brooklyn, NY 10010 (212) 834-6000

Sports officiating course.

LEE COLLEGE, Cleveland, TN 37311 (615) 472-2111

Officiating courses offered in team sports such as basketball, football and softball.

LOYOLA UNIVERSITY OF CHICAGO, 820 North Michigan Avenue, Chicago, IL 60611

Officiating courses in basketball and football.

MANCHESTER COLLEGE, North Manchester, IN 46962 (219) 982-2141

General officiating course.

UNIVERSITY OF MAINE AT FARMINGTON, Farmington, ME 04938

Course offered in field hockey umpiring.

MACALESTER COLLEGE, 1600 Grand Avenue, St. Paul, MN 55101 (612) 696-6357

General officiating course.

MARION COLLEGE, Marion, IN 46952

Officiating courses offered in volleyball, basketball, baseball, track & field.

MARQUETTE UNIVERSITY, 517 North 14th Street, Milwaukee, WI 53233

Coaching and officiating courses offered in basketball, football, volleyball, swimming, track & field.

MARYWOOD COLLEGE, 2300 Adams Avenue, Scranton, PA 18509

Officiating courses offered in basketball and field hockey.

MERCER UNIVERSITY ATLANTA, Atlanta, GA 30303 (404) 451-0331

Judging and officiating course.

MERCED COLLEGE, 3600 M Street, Carced, CA 95340

Officiating courses offered in football, cross country, soccer, water polo, wrestling, baseball, track & field, swimming, tennis, golf, volleyball, basketball and softball.

MIAMI-DADE COMMUNITY COLLEGE, New World Center Campus, 300 NE Second Avenue, Miami, FL 33176 577-6790

Officiating courses offered in football, basketball, baseball, track & field techniques.

UNIVERSITY OF MIAMI, Coral Gables, FL 33124

General officiating course.

MIAMI UNIVERSITY, Oxford, OH 45056 529-2161

Officiating courses offered in field hockey, basketball, volleyball and softball.

MIDWESTERN STATE UNIVERSITY, 3400 Taft Blvd., Wichita Falls, TX 76308 (817) 602-6611

Officiating courses offered in football, basketball.

MILLERSVILLE STATE COLLEGE, Millersville, PA 17551 Commonwealth of Pennsylvania

General officiating course.

MISSISSIPPI STATE UNIVERSITY, Mississippi State, MS 39762

Officiating major team sports (general).

MONTANA STATE UNIVERSITY, Bozeman, MT 59717

Officiating courses offered on football and basketball.

UNIVERSITY OF MONTANA, Missoula, MT 59801

Officiating courses include: basketball (women's and men's) and football.

MT. SAN ANTONIO COLLEGE, 1100 North Grand Avenue, Walnut, CA 91789 (714) 594-5611

Officiating courses include: basketball, volleyball, field hockey, softball, football, wrestling, soccer, baseball, track & field.

MUSKINGUM COLLEGE, New Concord, OH 43762

Officiating courses include: field hockey, football, basketball, volleyball, wrestling, baseball, softball, track & field.

NORWICH UNIVERSITY, Vermont College, Northfield, VT 05663

Officiating courses offered in team sports.

NORTHWESTERN COLLEGE, 3003 North Snelling Avenue, St. Paul, MN 55113 (612) 636-4840

Officiating courses offered in volleyball, football, basketball, baseball and softball.

NORTHWEST NAZARENE COLLEGE, Nampa, ID 83651

General officiating course.

NORTHERN STATE COLLEGE, Aberdeen, SD 57401

General officiating course emphasizing team sports.

NORTHERN MICHIGAN UNIVERSITY, Marguette, MI 49855 (906) 227-2650

General officiating course.

UNIVERSITY OF NORTHERN IOWA, Cedar Falls, IA 50613

Officiating courses include: basketball, field hockey, football, softball, swimming and volleyball.

NORTHERN ILLINOIS UNIVERSITY, Dekalb, IL 60115 (815) 753-0446

Officiating courses include: baseball/softball, field hockey, basketball, football, judging women's and men's gymnastics, competitive swimming and diving, track and field, volleyball.

UNIVERSITY OF NORTHERN COLORADO, Carter Hall 2012, Greeley, CO 80639

Officiating courses offered in baseball/softball, volleyball, tennis, gymnastics, basketball, wrestling, track and field, swimming, football.

NORTHERN ARIZONA UNIVERSITY, Box 4103, Flagstaff, AZ 86011 (602) 523-2108

Officiating fall sports for women's sports, field hockey, soccer, volleyball, basketball, and men's football.

UNIVERSITY OF NORTH DAKOTA, Box 8135, University Station, Grand Forts, ND 58202 (701) 777-2011

Officiating course offered in seasonal sports.

NORTH DAKOTA STATE UNIVERSITY, Fargo, ND 58102 (701) 237-8643

Officiating seasonal sports.

NORTH CAROLINA STATE UNIVERSITY, P.O. Box 5126, Raleigh, NC 27650 (919) 737-3409

Officiating courses offered in football, basketball, soccer, softball/ baseball and officiating intramural programs.

UNIVERSITY OF NORTH ALABAMA, Florence, Al 35630 (205) 766-4100 Ext. 318

Officiating courses offered in team, individual and dual sports.

OHIO UNIVERSITY, Athens, OH 45701

Officiating courses include football, basketball, baseball, track & field.

OREGON STATE UNIVERSITY, Corvallis, OR 97331

General officiating course.

OUR LADY OF HOLY CROSS COLLEGE, 4123 Woodland Drive, New Orleans, LA 70114

Officiating minor sports.

PEMBROKE STATE UNIVERSITY, Pembroke, NC 28372

Officiating courses include theory and techniques on football, soccer, wrestling, basketball, baseball, softball, track & field, field hockey, tennis and volleyball.

THE PENNSYLVANIA STATE UNIVERSITY, 210 Shields Building, University Park, PA 16802

Officiating courses include football, field hockey and soccer, volleyball, wrestling, basketball, gymnastics.

POINT LOMA COLLEGE, 3900 Lomaland Drive, San Diego, CA 92106 (714) 222-6474

General officiating theory and practice course.

PORTLAND STATE UNIVERSITY, P.O. Box 751, Portland, OR 97207 (503) 229-4081

General officiating course.

UNIVERSITY OF PUGET SOUND, 1500 North Warner Street, Tacoma, WA 98416

Officiating courses include techniques and methods of officiating volleyball, soccer, football and wrestling, basketball, swimming, baseball, track & field.

PURDUE UNIVERSITY, West LaFayette, IN 47907 (219) 844-0520

Officiating courses include football, basketball, wrestling, track & field, volleyball, softball, swimming and gymnastics.

ROCKFORD COLLEGE, Rockford, IL 61101 (815) 226-4000

Officiating course on football, basketball, track & field, soccer, volleyball and baseball.

ROCKHURST COLLEGE, 5225 Troost Avenue, Kansas City, MO 64110 926-4100

General officiating course.

ST. CLOUD STATE UNIVERSITY, St. Cloud, MN 56301

Officiating courses include men's football and basketball, and women's softball, basketball and volleyball.

SALISBURY STATE COLLEGE, Salisbury, MD 21801 (301) 546-3261

Courses offered in both coaching and officiating sports. Courses include field hockey, basketball, volleyball, softball, tennis, football, soccer, wrestling.

SAN JOSE CITY COLLEGE, 2100 Moorpark Avenue, San Jose CA 95128 (408) 998-1147

Officiating course offered in football, basketball, baseball, basketball and volleyball.

SINCLAIR COMMUNITY COLLEGE, 444 West Third Street, Dayton, OH 45402

Officiating courses offered in basketball, football and baseball.

SOUTH DAKOTA STATE UNIVERSITY, Box 2201, Brookings, SD 57007

Coaching and officiating of general athletics.

SOUTHEAST MISSOURI STATE UNIVERSITY, Cape Girardeau, MO 63701 (314) 651-2000

Officiating courses offered in basketball, volleyball, baseball, softball, track & field, field hockey, wrestling, football.

SOUTHERN CALIFORNIA COLLEGE, 55 Fair Drive, Costa Mesa, CA 92626 (714) 556-3610

General officiating course.

SOUTHERN CALIFORNIA UNIVERSITY, P.O. Box 77952, Los Angeles, CA 90007 (213) 743-7360

Principles of officiating basketball and volleyball.

SOUTHERN COLORADO UNIVERSITY, Pueblo, CO 81001

General officiating course.

SOUTHERN CONNECTICUT STATE COLLEGE, 501 Crescent Street, New Haven, CT 06515 (203) 397-4000

Officiating courses include field hockey, swimming, basketball, gymnastics, volleyball, track & field.

SOUTHERN OREGON STATE COLLEGE, Ashland, OR 97520 (503) 482-3311

Officiating courses include football, basketball, baseball, track & field, wrestling, gymnastics, aquatics.

SOUTHERN UTAH STATE COLLEGE, Cedar City, UT 84720 (801) 586-7700

Officiating courses offered in basketball, football, baseball, track, volleyball and softball.

SOUTHWEST STATE UNIVERSITY, Marshall, MN 56258

Officiating courses offered in basketball, football, gymnastics, swimming and volleyball.

SOUTHWEST TEXAS STATE UNIVERSITY, San Marcos, TX 78666 (512) 245-2364

Officiating courses offered in volleyball, handball, softball, touch football, soccer and tumbling.

STILLMAN COLLEGE, Tuscaloosa, AL 35401

Coaching and officiating courses in football, baseball, basketball, track & field.

TAYLOR UNIVERSITY, Upland, IN 46989 (317) 998-2751

Officiating course in men's and women's sports.

TENNESSEE TEMPLE UNIVERSITY, 1815 Union Avenue, Chattanooga, TN 37404 (615) 698-6021

General course in rules and officiating.

TEXAS A & I UNIVERSITY, Kingsville, TX 78363 (512) 595-2111

Intramural officiating.

TEXAS A & M UNIVERSITY, College Station, TX 77843

Officiating course includes football, soccer, swimming and water polo, basketball, baseball/softball, wrestling, track & field.

OKLAHOMA STATE UNIVERSITY, Stillwater, OK 74074 (405) 624-5200

General officiating course.

THE SCHOOL OF THE OZARKS, Point Lookout, MO 65726 (417) 334-6411

General men's and women's officiating course.

PITTSBURG STATE UNIVERSITY, Pittsburg, KS 66762 (316) 231-7000

Rules and officiating courses (general).

UNIVERSITY OF TEXAS AT ARLINGTON, Box 19088 U.T.A. Station, Arlington, TX 76019

Officiating men's and women's sports.

TRINITY UNIVERSITY, San Antonio, TX 78284 (512) 736-7207

General officiating courses.

UTAH STATE UNIVERSITY, Logan, UT 84321 (801) 750-1923

Officiating courses in football and volleyball.

THE VICTORIA COLLEGE, 2200 East Red River Street, Victoria, TX 77901

Officiating studies include football, basketball, track, volleyball and softball.

WAYNE STATE COLLEGE, Wayne, NE 68787 (402) 375-2200

General officiating course.

WASHBURN UNIVERSITY OF TOPEKA, Topeka, KS 66621 (913) 295-6300

General officiating courses.

WAYNE STATE UNIVERSITY, 5980 Cass Avenue, Detroit, MI 48202

Officiating courses include baseball, basketball, football and volleyball.

WASHINGTON & LEE UNIVERSITY, Lexington, VA 24450 (703) 463-9111 Ext. 203

General officiating course.

WEST VIRGINIA WESLEYAN COLLEGE, Buckhannan, WV 26201 (304) 473-7011

Officiating courses include football, track & field, basketball and baseball.

WEST TEXAS STATE UNIVERSITY, Canyon, TX 79016

Officiating course in football, plus men's and women's officiating courses in basketball, baseball and softball.

WEBER STATE COLLEGE, Ogden, UT 84408 (801) 626-6000

Officiating courses in volleyball, basketball, softball.

WESTERN NEW MEXICO UNIVERSITY, Silver City, NM 88061

Officiating courses in football and basketball.

WESTERN MONTANA COLLEGE, Dillon, MT 59725

Officiating courses in basketball, volleyball, football, wrestling.

WESTERN MICHIGAN UNIVERSITY, Kalamazoo, MI 49001 (616) 383-1600

Officiating courses in basketball, football, field hockey, volleyball, baseball.

WEST VIRGINIA UNIVERSITY, Morgantown, WV 26506

General officiating course.

WESTERN STATE COLLEGE OF COLORADO, Gunnison, CO 81230 943-2119

Officiating courses in football, volleyball, wrestling, basketball, gymnastics, baseball, track & field.

UNIVERSITY OF WISCONSIN, Eau Claire, WI 54701

Officiating courses in basketball, women's track & field, women's volleyball and women's gymnastics.

UNIVERSITY OF WISCONSIN, Green Bay, WI 54302

Officiating courses include basketball, field hockey, football, gymnastics, baseball/softball, swimming/diving, volleyball, wrestling.

WRIGHT STATE UNIVERSITY, Dayton, OH 45435 (513) 873-2975

Officiating courses include basketball, baseball, football, soccer and volleyball.

YOUNGSTOWN STATE UNIVERSITY, Youngstown, OH 44555

Officiating courses include soccer, basketball, football, track & field, volleyball, swimming, gymnastics, baseball, field hockey.

APPENDIX F

SPORTS EQUIPMENT MANUFACTURERS AND SUPPLIERS

Aspiring officials should acquire the best equipment available. There is no excuse for any official to appear at a job without the necessary equipment. Being properly equipped can make the difference in the official's performance. The following manufacturers and suppliers distribute the latest in equipment for officials. You may want to contact a few of the following companies and request either a catalogue or price sheet prior to purchasing equipment.

SPORTS ACCESSORIES, INC., 15801-T Gaither Dr., Gaithersburg, MD 20760 (301) 948-9610

SPORTS EQUIPMENT, INC., 723-TS 2nd St., Greenville, IL 62246 (618) 664-2250

SPORTS EDUCATIONAL DEVICES CO., P.O. Box 386, Corona Del Mar, CA 92625 (714) 673-8617

SPORTS STYLES, INC., 510 No. Madison, Rockford, IL 61107 (815) 963-6615 (Uniforms, caps, hats, visors)

SPORTS TOURE INDUSTRIES CORP., 678-T Berriman, Brooklyn, NY 11208 (212) 649-7000.

SPOT-BILT, INC. (Hyde Athletic Industries), Farm Rd., Bangor, ME 04401 (207) 942-5222

OLYMPIAN SPORTS EQUIPMENT, 1200-T Firestone Pky., Akron, OH

OFFICIAL STOCK BALL BAT (Idemn Mfg. Co.), 160 Jay, Brooklyn, NY (212) 855-1303

SPORT STAR AMARREAN, 15 Sauer St., Wave, MA (Athletic Shoes)

SPORTCRAFT SPORTING GOODS (General Sportcraft Co., Ltd.) 140 Woodbone St., Barganfield, NY (210) 384-4242

SPORTS ATHLETIC FACILITY PRODUCTS, CBF INDUSTRIES, INC., 10414 Harry Hines Blvd., Dallas, TX

SPORTLINE SPORTING GOODS, HOMEMAKER INDUSTRIES, INC., 3300 W. Franklin Blvd., Chicago, IL (312) 722-3100

SPORTMASTER, STOP CLOCK, Merit Watch Co., Inc., 630 Fifth Ave., New York, NY (212) 247-3118

SPORTSMAN ATHLETIC HOSIERY, Wm H. Horn & Bro., Inc., 451 N. 3rd, Philadelphia, PA (215) 627-2773

WORLD SPORTING GOOD, Inc. 1306-T St Stephens Rd., Mobile, AL (205) 438-4676 (football equipment)

MARCY GYMNASIUM EQUIPMENT CO., 1732-36 Standard Ave., Glendale, CA (213) 247-6611 (athletic equipment)

LOGAN, INC., 16952 Milliken Ave., Irvine, CA (714) 556-6441 (athletic equipment)

SUPERIOR SPORTS FABRICATORS, ENTERPRISES, INC., 746-T W. Algonquin Rd., Arlington Hts., IL (312) 364-0707 (hockey equipment, guards, blister pads)

MEVCO SCOREBOARD CO., 223 E. Harris Ave., Greenville, IL (618) 664-0360 (scoreboards, sports timing equipment)

RAWLINGS SPORTING GOODS, 2300 Delmar, St. Louis, MO 63103 (314) 241-2900

ATHLETIC, INC., Dept TR P.O. Box 521, Columbus, NE (402) 564-5810 (athletic equipment)

SPORTING GOODS MANUFACTURERS ASSOCIATION, 200 Castlewood Dr., North Palm Beach, FL 33408 (305) 842-4100

GENERAL SPORTING GOODS CORP., Gardner, MA 01440 (617) 623-0620

SUPERIOR SPORTS PRODUCTS, 706 S. State, Litchfield, IL (217) 324-5965 (football & basketball jerseys)

UAN GINKEL ATHLETIC MFG. CO., 2208 Ingersoll, Des Moines, IA (512) 244-7718 (athletic garments)

SPALDING, 425-T Meadow St., Chicopee, MA (413) 536-1200 (full line of sporting goods)

KUMBAK CO., 6855-T Oxford St., St. Louis Park, MN 55426 (612) 929-0325 (campass match case & whistles)

JACK ESSES DISTRIBUTING CO., 1627 Washington Ave., St. Louis, MO 63103 (800) 325-7178 (athletic clothing, equipment, shoes for all sports and seasons)

ARISTO CO., INC., 51 Rockefeller Plaza, New York, NY 10020 (212) 247-0720 (stop watches, sports timers, pedometers)

INDUSTRIAL TIME CORP, Dept. R, 599 5th Ave., New York, NY (212) 751-2926 (stop watches)

DUCOMMUN MFG CO., INC., 56-58 Main St., Warwich, NY 10990 (914) 986-6757 (heavy duty stop watches)

ROYAL TEXTILE MILLS, INC., 223-T N. First St., Yanceyville, NC (919) 694-4121 (elbow & knee pads, supporters)

HUTCH SPORTING GOODS, INC., 1924 W. 8th St., Cincinnati, OH (513) 251-4510 (football, basketball, baseball, soccer, boxing equipment)

JUNG PRODUCTS, INC., 5801 Mariemont Ave., Cincinnati, OH (513) 271-3400 (forearm & knee pads, hand protectors, trainer's packs)

S. E. HYMAN CO., P.O. Box 587, Fremont, OH (419) 332-7315 (sports wear & insulated underwear)

AMERICAN BASEBALL CAP, Inc., 310-T Median Station Rd., Media, PA (215) 565-0945 (hats & caps)

DAVIS & BOX MFG CO., INC., 10950 Shady Trail, Dallas, TX (214) 350-1092 (score books, football tees)

BILL KELLEY ATHLETIC, INC., 921-TS Great Southwest Pky., Grant Prairie, TX (214) 641-2556 (protective equipment)

TEXACE DIVISION OF A-T-O, INC., 402 W. Mueua St., San Antonio, TX (512) 227-7551 (caps & hats)

SAFE-T-GUARD, INC., 6911 Raywood Rd., Madison, WI (608) 222-5542 (mouth pieces, guards, face masks, eyeglass holders, soccer shin guards)

ADLAR'S SPORTING GOODS WAREHOUSE, 222 Alpha Park, Cleveland, OH (216) 442-0980

ALL-SPORT, 229 So. Court, Medina, OH (216) 725-8110

AMERICAN ATHLETIC, INC., 1062 Jacoby RD, Copley, OH (216) 666-0511

BRUELL C T WHOLESALE SPORTING GOODS CO., 470 Portage Lakes Dr., Akron, OH (216) 644-2259

FAIRLORN ENTERPRISES, INC., 1190 Ranchland Dr., Cleveland, OH (216) 473-1090

SPORTS PRODUCTS CORP., 4701 Manufacturing, Cleveland, OH (216) 267-6540

SUPERIOR SPORTS WARE HOUSE, 1549 Superior Ave., Cleveland, OH (216) 241-3150

TUFFY PAD CO., 454 Seasons, Akron, OH (216) 688-0043

MEYER, INC., 46 East 20th St., New York, NY 10003 (213) 533-1000 (uniforms & whistles)

M & B HEADWEAR CO., INC., 2323 E. Main St., Richmond, Va 23223 (804) 648-1603

SHAFFER SPORTSWEAR MFG., INC. 1003-T So. Main St., Bentonville, AR (501) 273-9525

EDWARD HYMAN CO., 6311-T DeSoto Ave., Woodland Hills, Ca (213) 992-7611 (professional uniforms & accessories)

GARBAR MFG. CO., INC., Harrison & Beigar St., Mishawaka, IN (219) 259-2481

ACE UNIFORMS CO., 203-T Market, Newark, NJ (201) 622-2211 (all types of uniforms)

FASHION SEAL UNIFORMS DIV., 63 New York Ave., Huntington, NY (516) 427-7400

ATHLETIC KNITWEAR MFG CO., INC., 745 West 25th St., Hialeah, FL (305) 888-4538 (soccer)

WILSON SPORTING GOODS CO., 2233 West St., River Grove, IL (312) 456-6100 (baseball, football, basketball, softball, soccer)

DELANG SPORTSWEAR, INC., P.O. Box 270, Grinnell, IA (512) 236-6145 (baseball)

COLLEGE BOWL, INC., 333-T W. Baltimore St., Baltimore, MD (301) 685-0661

STALL & DEAN MFG. CO., 95 Church St., Brockton, MA (617) 586-2414 (baseball, softball & hockey)

EVERLAST SPORTING GOODS MFG. CO, INC., 750 East 132nd St., Bronx, NY (212) 993-0100

GIBRALTAR INDUSTRIES, INC., 254 36th St., Bldg 2, Brooklyn, NY (212) 965-6666

EMPIRE SPORTING GOODS MFG. CO., 443 Broadway, New York, NY (212) 966-0880

FELCO ATHLETIC WEAR CO., 113 4th Ave., New York, NY (212) 533-8700

STYLECRAFT MANUFACTURING CO., 205-T West 4th, Cincinnati, OH (513) 721-6722 (baseball caps)

GENERAL ATHLETIC PRODUCTS CO., Greenville, OH (513) 548-4131

MAPLE MFG. CO., INC., 1309-T Moble St., Philadelphia, PA (215) 925-2314

FAB-KNIT MFG. CO., 1415-T North 4th St., Waco, TX (817) 754-0367

RUSSELL CORP, P.O. Box 272, Alexander City, AL (205) 234-4251 (uniforms & apparel)

E. R. MOORE CO., 7230 No. Caldwell, Niles, IL (312) 647-7950 (team uniforms)

POWERS MFG. CO., 1340 Sycarmore, Waterloo, IA (319) 233-6118 (uniforms)

ADVER-TEK, INC., 854 Angliana Ave., Lexington, KY (606) 253-2671

MECA SPORTSWEAR, INC., 2363-T University Ave., St. Paul, MN (612) 646-4886 (football & soccer)

PACIFIC ATHLETIC CO., 14501 So. Figueroa St., Gardena, CA (213) 321-8511 (sportswear)

KOTZIN, TOBIAS CO., 1300 Santee, Los Angeles, CA (213) 749-0251 (men's slacks & taps, sportswear)

F. BRODY & SONS, CO., 312 Court, Des Moines, IA (515) 288-7451 (men's slacks)

GENERAL UNIFORMS CORP., 1127-T Woodmere Ave., Traverse City, MI (616) 946-1713 (uniforms, trousers, shirts, caps, hats and accessories)

SERON MFG. CO., 254 Republic Ave., Joliet, IL (815) 725-1502

W.S. DARLEY & CO., 2000 Anson Dr., Melrose Park, IL (312) 345-8050

CLARK-COOPER CORP., 464 No. Randolph Ave., Cinaminson, NJ (609) 829-4580

WESTMINISTER SPORTS, INC., 32-21 Downing St., Flushing, NY (212) 762-8300 (brass & chrome whistles)

AXELROD CO., INC., 9 West 30th St., New York, NY (212) 594-3022 (whistles)

SUAVE SHOE CORP., 14100 NW 60th Ave., Miami Lakes, FL (305) 822-7880 (sneakers, basketball & deck shoes)

RIDDELL, INC., 1001 East Touhy, Des Plaines, IL (312) 299-4030 (football & baseball shoes)

HYDE ATHLETIC INDUSTRIES, INC., 432 Columbus St., Cambridge, MA (617) 547-9210 (full range of footgear)

BROOKS SHOE MFG. CO., Factory & Terrace Sts., Hanover, PA (717) 632-1755 (shoes for baseball, basketball, football and soccer)

SPORTS OFFICIATING SUPPLIES (SOS), 19325 Saticoy St., Reseda, CA 91325 (800) 423-5004 in CA: 882-0281 (wide range of umpire supplies)

TOM ALLEN ENTERPRISES, 3117 Merriam Lane, Kansas City, KS 66106 (800) 255-6277 in KS: 262-3734 (wide range of professional supplies & equipment)

NATIONAL FEDERATIONS OF STATE HIGH SCHOOL ASSOCIATIONS, 11724 Plaza Circle, P.O. Box 20626, Kansas City, MO 64195 (scorebooks, sports video cassettes) Items must be ordered by mail — no phone number.